KILLING BOBBY R.

KILLING BOBBY R.

AN ADAM MANSHIP INQUIRY

JAMES L. WILSON

October Light Publishing Co.

OTHER BOOKS BY THIS AUTHOR:

Clementine Hunter, American Folk Artist; Pelican Publishing
The Charm and Other Stories; October Light Publishing Co.

Published by October Light Publishing Co.

ISBN 978-1-7323897-0-0

Typesetting services by BOOKOW.COM

For Mar'Sue

PROLOGUE

On Easter Sunday, 1988, Robert 'Bobby' Rollings, Jr., a wealthy young Atlanta investment banker, was murdered at his weekend home just outside the small town of New Bethany, Georgia.

I was a reporter for *The Atlanta Democrat* at the time and was assigned to cover the killing. Though I had worked for the paper for seven years, this assignment was a first for me: It came with orders not to print a word.

Those orders had come directly from the top, from our owner and publisher, Adam Manship.

As the mystery unraveled, it revealed a web of tangled loyalties and twisted hearts. It became a story of tragic proportions. But it was one story Mr. Manship would not allow told during his lifetime.

This story began my long association with this most remarkable man. What followed was twenty-five years as head of his personal, in-house intelligence team. Our assignments were always the stories – or *inquiries* as Mr. Manship preferred to call them – that he wanted to pursue for his own reasons. On the quiet. Never for publication. For his purposes only.

We never asked him why. But almost always, as in this first inquiry, what we uncovered would answer that question.

–Gil Coates
Atlanta, Georgia
July, 2014

1

EASTER SUNDAY, 1988.

The highway was dark and desolate, lit only by a pale moon. Patches of pre-dawn mist had settled on the road and across the fields, over the occasional farmhouse or shanty.

Ronnie Lee Brown kept the windows of the old yellow Cadillac he drove rolled up tight as he pushed deep into the mist. The mist spooked him. The old car groaned, the tires whistled, the floorboard creaked. He could hear the shotgun bumping around on the rear floorboard, the handful of shells he'd been given rolling side to side.

He slumped low in the seat and pulled his watch cap down to his eyes. Sweat beaded on his lip. His big, rugged hands clung tight to the wheel. Just ahead, he knew, there was a four or five mile stretch where he could push the Caddy to a hundred, maybe a hundred and ten if it didn't start rattling out of control. He had to be in place by sunrise, that was the deal.

He reached up, pulled the sweat off his lip with his forefinger, then pointed it straight down the road.

"I'm doing this shit now right now, and it don't matter about the rest," he shouted to himself. He slammed the heel of his hand on the wheel then clamped his fingers around it. He wrung it hard. He stared ahead and repeated, in a whisper this time, "I'm doing this shit right now, the rest don't matter."

He saw a ghostly figure in the road ahead. He blinked the headlights rapidly. He rubbed his eyes, mashed them closed and shook his head. As he got closer, he saw it was only a wisp of morning fog. He jammed the gas and plowed into it.

The old Caddy popped out of the other side as if it was spit out. He was doing over a hundred now. The car shook, vibrated and whined. The shotgun bounced around in the floorboard, thumped into the back of the driver's seat.

Brown rolled his window down and felt the rush of cold, black air. He drew a deep breath, closed his eyes for an instant and pressed the gas to the floor. He lunged into the mist again and seemed to disappear.

A half hour later he had pulled the car off the side of a small dark road and was walking fast, shotgun in his right hand, poking down like a walking stick. The dark dawn, the quiet, the stillness were terrifying to him, made worse knowing what he was supposed to do. Still, he moved on.

He turned off the road into woods that ran alongside the Bobby Rollings estate. He clicked on a flashlight and pushed his way silently through the woods. In a moment, he began to see a flicker of light – the security light at the rear of the house – and clicked off the flashlight.

The woods began to thin and he could see the tree line surrounding the house. There was a spacious lawn at the rear and some fifty yards away, a large patio area connected to the back of the house. Down to his right and just feet from the tree line was a tarp-covered woodpile. He moved quickly to behind the woodpile and sat down. He laid the shotgun across his lap and fixed his eyes on the house.

At first light there was a stirring in the house. Several lights came on inside, then an outside light across the patio.

Bobby Rollings emerged from the patio door in a heavy blue robe and floppy slippers. He appeared drowsy, still half-asleep. He shivered, looked around for a moment. He was carrying an Easter basket heaped with colorful eggs and began looking for spots to hide them. He placed a few here, a few there, in plain sight on the patio. He put one on the seat of a small red tricycle. He stepped off the patio, onto the lawn and headed toward the rear tree line.

Brown was suddenly confused, his heart pounding. This wasn't right – Rollings was supposed to be going the other way, up his front drive toward the road to get the morning paper. He squirmed around, eased up onto his knees, keeping the shotgun low.

The sky was lighter now, and Rollings moved further to the back of the lawn, hiding eggs in more difficult spots, pointing at each with a finger, fixing its place in his mind. Abruptly, he spun and headed toward the woodpile.

"Shit, he's comin' right to me," Brown whispered to himself. His mind was a blur. What the shit? What the hell am I supposed to do? Shoot him now? Shoot him in the back when he turns? Oh shit….

Another light came on in the house. Then another.

Brown was near panic, but panic or no, he knew he couldn't stop now. Too late for that – once you take the money, you're in.

Rollings was almost to the woodpile. Every few steps, he'd stop, stoop, slide an egg under a fallen limb, slip one between tufts of grass.

Brown rose silently and began stepping back from the woodpile, toward the tree line, fingering the shotgun, taking it in both hands. He was suddenly on the defensive. He backed away further, faster. He stepped on a limb and stumbled.

Bobby Rollings raised his eyes to the noise and saw a figure in the shadowy tree line. It was clearly a man, but he couldn't see detail.

Then the figure pulled something up – what was it, a gun, a rifle? – and held it chest high, pointed at him.

"Who's there?" said Rollings.

The figure froze. Rollings froze.

"Hey, who's there?" he called again. He glanced back toward his house, then back to the figure. The figure stepped forward, and Rollings could see him more clearly.

"Hey, fella, come on out from there." Rollings saw the shotgun. "What the hell are you doing with that?"

A door slammed back at the house. Out came a small, blond-haired boy carrying an Easter basket and rubbing his eyes, calling out, "Daddy? Where are you? Daddy?"

Rollings swung his head back toward the boy, "Son, get back in the house. Get back inside right now."

"Daddy. Daddy." The boy stumbled toward the sound of his father's voice. "He came! The Easter bunny came! He came!"

"Get back inside, Robert!" Rollings screamed. "Go inside right now." He turned back to the man with the shotgun. "Look, fella…"

Brown charged at him wildly, thrust the shotgun in his face, and pulled the trigger. Once. Twice. Bobby Rollings' head exploded. His body spilled to the ground.

"Daddy? Daddy?" The boy stopped moving and looked around. He turned back toward the house, then back to that horrible noise. He stood waiting, waiting to be told what to do. In a moment, he started moving toward his father's body.

Ronnie Lee Brown broke into a full run, straight for the road, past the boy, across the lawn, up the drive and out onto the blacktop. He ran as fast as he'd ever run in his life.

He could run faster without the shotgun, he thought. Then he remembered – not yet, don't throw the gun away yet. "Go, run," he barked to himself with each pounding step. In a moment, he was back on the road where he'd left the car. In the next moment he was inside the car telling himself what was next, "Now go! You gotta go. Gotta go. Back the way you came."

He spun the car around and tore away.

Not ten minutes later he had stopped the car on the Highway 37 bridge that crossed the Flint River. He stepped quickly to the railing and threw the shotgun into the dark, tumbling waters below.

He did not see, as he hurried back into the car, the old man in the gray utility van who had pulled off on a side road just below the bridge to relieve himself.

2

WITHIN an hour of the shooting I was on my way out of Atlanta headed south to the scene.

I'd been called by our weekend editor, Calvin Daniels, who had given me the victim's name, directions to the crime scene and some strange orders. They had come straight from the top, from the owner and publisher, Adam Manship.

"Get down there as fast as you can, get everything you can, then report to him at his house tonight," Daniels had said. "Do *not* file a story. Don't call anything in. Take whatever you get straight to him."

He added that Manship had named me specifically for the job.

I say these were strange orders because at the time, Mr. Manship knew me as a City Hall reporter. If he knew me at all. I had met him, only briefly, twice. The first time was in my employment interview seven years earlier. He'd stayed in the interview five minutes, asked one innocuous question and then hurried from the room, saying "Welcome aboard." Two suits finished the interview and signed me up.

I'd met him the second time four months ago, when I presented to him, my editors, and the paper's lawyers all the support I had for a big, ugly story. It accused the Atlanta City Administrator, Julian Makar, and three of his underlings, of looting more than $5.7 million from city coffers. It was a hydra-headed scandal that both state and federal investigators had been circling for months. I had everything they had – more than enough to break the story. I was sure arrests were imminent. Mr. Manship ordered the story held until arrests were made. So far there hadn't been any.

Calvin Daniels didn't understand today's orders either. He'd never been called directly by Manship, never been asked by him to cover a specific story. The truth was, none of us ever saw Mr. Manship around the paper. His name was rarely mentioned by our editors. He'd never intervened anywhere that I'd heard of. We assumed he had more pressing matters than the day-to-day of the *Atlanta Democrat*.

"What the hell, a shooting in Podunk? When was this again?"

"Crack of dawn, less than an hour ago."

"Damn, Calvin, I haven't pulled a police call in years," I yelled into the phone as I gathered my gear. "Is this some kind of god-damn demotion or something?"

"Might be, Coates. I hear you've been a pisshead around here since they killed your Makar story," he said. "Hey, I'm looking at the roster, aren't you supposed to be off this weekend?"

"Hell yes."

"Too bad. Now you're not. Sorry," he said.

"I can tell it's breaking you're heart. What do I do, call him when I get back?"

"He gave me his private number, so yeah, call him. Oh, and look, Coates, so we're absolutely clear on this. . . this is strictly off the books. You got that? That's what the boss says. Him, you, me – that's the entire universe on this. Got it?"

"I got it, I got it."

"Good. So you're wasting time, get your ass down to Latham County, pronto."

3

I⊤ was bright and cold that Sunday morning. The sun held that orange glow it always had when it peered, fiery and one-eyed, into the day ahead. I don't know what it saw in store for me, but Easter Sunday, 1988, wasn't going to be a good one for the family of Bobby Rollings.

I made it from Atlanta to Latham County in less than an hour. The crime scene would still be hot. This was a small, rural community, it was a Sunday morning, and these country cops with little homicide experience would be slow to organize, get the coroner out, call the DA – all the things the law makes you do on a crime like this. My bet was the body would still be around somewhere and no one clearly in charge.

In chaos is opportunity.

I found the road – Pine Hill Road – that Daniels told me to look for. It was about ten miles off the Interstate, a well-groomed black-top discreetly tucked away in a rolling mix of pines and hardwoods. I turned onto the road and slowed immediately.

At the far end, maybe a half mile down, was a cul-de-sac packed with patrol cars, dark Crown Vics, an ambulance and a couple of state trooper cars.

There were a half-dozen homes along the road – large, expensive places gussied up as antebellum estates, each set back among the trees, barely in view from the road. At the very end, off to the right of all the cars and down a long deep slope, sat a sprawling, sharply angled, contemporary house. The entire lot was circled in police tape.

I pulled to the side of the road behind a cop car and parked. Down the way, a deputy was escorting an old man in a tan jumpsuit across the road to a gray utility van. The cop was patting him on the back, nodding appreciatively and obviously trying to move him on.

The old man climbed slowly into his van and pulled away. As he rolled past me I noted the sign on the side: "Carrier 1515, *New Bethany Times*."

A delivery guy for the local paper. Maybe a witness to something. I made a note to track him down later in the day.

The deputy spotted me and walked to my car.

"Can I help you?" he said, standing stiff-legged and straight-backed, his hand covering the gun on his hip. He had a military haircut and wore mirrored sunglasses. His facial features hardly moved. I guessed he was about my age, early thirties. The name plate on his khaki shirt said "Weaver."

"Gil Coates with the *Atlanta Democrat*." I handed him my press card. "Boss sent me down to get some info."

The cop studied my card then handed it back with a flat smile.

"Our first reporter of the day. You got here fast – how do you boys do that?"

I shrugged and stepped out of the car. "We never sleep. Who can I talk to?"

"Chief Deputy Will Black is in charge. Maybe the DA, technically. Both down there."

I glanced over his shoulder toward all the uniforms milling around the house. There were a half-dozen standing on the front gallery, looking at one another. The massive two-storied front door stood wide open.

I sidestepped the deputy to get a better look behind the house. The body was still there at the rear of the back lawn, covered. Two men in windbreakers, hands in their pockets, stood over it, talking.

"Is that the Chief Deputy down by the body? And the coroner?"

"That's right," Weaver said without looking.

"Can I talk to one of them?"

"Not a good time." He shifted his stance stiffly.

"I'll wait up here for one of them."

"It's a crime scene down there. Off limits."

"Like I said, right here."

The deputy slid his glasses off and eyed me, probably doubting he could take me at my word.

"How far into town from here?" I asked.

"New Bethany's about five miles."

"That's the County Seat?"

"Correct."

"This'll be the Sheriff's jurisdiction?"

"Right. We'll be handling this…Sheriff Fowler will, that is. He's away for now, Chief Black is in charge. That's who you need to talk to, not anyone else." He lifted a warning finger.

I nodded.

The town of New Bethany, population about 7,500, was the hub of Latham County. The rest of the county was made of small farming communities, small family spreads and a few large operating plantations, mostly corporate owned. The main crops in this part of Georgia were cotton and soybean.

Back in the day when cotton was king, Latham County and the entire lower Flint River had been prime agricultural real estate. In recent times it had become the site of country homes for Atlanta's rich, young and restless.

There was a surge of activity down at the scene.

The Chief Deputy and the Coroner had broken away from the body and were walking back up toward the rear of the house. Two EMTs had loaded the body on a gurney and were rolling it up toward the ambulance on the road. One of the cops on the front gallery whistled to Weaver and waved him down.

"You'll need to stay put for now," he said sternly. He eyed me a moment more then hurried across the long sloping lawn to the house.

I stepped down the road to the ambulance and showed my press badge to the two EMTs as they were about to load the body. "Is that Mr. Rollings?"

One glared and said nothing. The other muttered, "No comment."

"Can I see the body?"

"I just said no comment."

"He was shot, right? Where? What was it?"

"No comment, again," he barked.

One thing you learn quickly in this business, if you want to stay in it, is to keep asking questions until somebody makes you stop.

"A quick look, fellas, no camera?" I asked.

The first EMT stopped what he was doing and glared, "Look, buddy, you might think you want to see this, but you don't. Take my word for it."

"I live in Atlanta. We're used to dead bodies," I said.

He looked away and thought for a second, maybe wondering if the only way he was going to get rid of me was to give me something. He would be right.

"Bad ain't the word for it," he said, looking back. "Two shots in the face, up close. A shotgun it looks like. Not much left of him. Now move out of the way. And that was off the record, by the way," he quickly added.

I moved aside and nodded thanks, though he never saw it.

Strictly speaking, when someone adds "oh yeah, that was off the record" after blabbing something he shouldn't have, I don't have to honor it. But most times I do, and I would in this case. No need to cause these guys any grief with the cops.

I lit a cigarette and stood watching the house, looking for something to inspire my next move.

The deputy had asked a good question. How *did* I get there so fast? When Daniels called me, the shooting had occurred less than an hour before. Mr. Manship had called *him* before that. So that meant Manship knew about it no more than thirty minutes after it happened. How was that?

Some guy is killed in some backwater an hour outside Atlanta on a Sunday morning and Adam Manship, the billionaire owner of a media empire, knows about it within minutes? Who told him? Why would he care? And why send me, or anyone else for that matter, down from Atlanta when the paper had stringers in every county?

I figured I would find all that out when I met with him.

I stomped the cigarette and looked again at the crime scene. The sun had lifted above the tree line and threw slashes of light across the grounds – handsome, well-manicured grounds with little azalea groves tossed here and there. The house itself was a statement. It said: "We ain't kidding about how much money we have."

As I surveyed the place, I saw that all the cops had disappeared. There was no one outside the house, front or back. Their cars were all still there, empty. Must be some kind of powwow inside.

I looked again to be sure I wasn't missing the stray cop in the woods or back near that woodpile where the body had been.

I saw no one.

So, I did what I usually did when left unattended, I went looking for someone to talk to.

The ground where the body had laid was saturated in blood. Oddly, it hadn't been taped off or marked in any way. A few steps away was a woodpile with signs of fresh stirrings on one side: trampled grass, a mashed pine cone, something that might have been a footprint. A dozen steps further, at the edge of the tree line, were orange crime-scene flags stuck beside obvious footprints – possibly the killer's.

As I moved to the rear of the house, I noticed how quiet and still it was. That, along with the fact that I was able to move freely around the crime scene, with no sign of a cop anywhere, gave me an uneasy feeling. Not enough to stop me, but uneasy nonetheless.

I heard voices up on the road, then car doors slamming, cars beginning to roll through the gravel. They were moving out; they'd been assembled in the house, no doubt, to go over their next moves.

The curtains were drawn in back, across a span of floor-to-ceiling glass that ran almost the entire width of the house. Attached to the house was a long, wide patio of gray flagstone, scattered with toys. There was a kid's tricycle with an Easter egg in the seat. I could see a line of small bloody footprints crossing from the lawn over toward a rear door. They were dry to the touch, and, again, not marked by the cops. An Easter basket laid spilled on its side near the door.

There were voices coming from inside – a man and a woman, muted but argumentative. I eased a few steps closer. The woman was alternately hysterical and shrill, then guttural and groaning. She was saying something about her grandfather, something about his wishes, something about "little Robert."

After a long silence she said, clearly, with a heavy sigh, "Oh Bobby, oh Bobby, oh Bobby."

There was a sliver of an opening in the curtains and I peeked in. A tall, raven-haired woman stood at the end of a sofa in a pale blue robe. The front of the robe was partially open and splotched with blood. She stood calmly, almost regally, smoking a cigarette and gazing, as if in a trance, at a man in a dark blue suit standing right in front of her.

The man tried to reach out and put a comforting hand on her shoulder. She avoided the move with a subtle twist. Beside the woman, clinging to her leg, stood a small, blond-headed boy, his face buried in her robe.

Though her long hair was a tangled mess and her eyes ringed with the dark stains of tragedy, she was a stunning woman. She seemed to possess a dangerous magnetism, the kind of attraction that made the perils she almost certainly brought with her seem irrelevant. This was the lady of the house, no doubt – the victim's wife.

As I eased back and turned to leave, I came nose-to-nose with a large, red-eyed cop with a sour stare. He was mostly unkempt and wore a rumpled khaki uniform with an ample belly spilling over the belt. His shaggy gray hair surrounded a face fallen into tired, fleshy rolls.

He glanced at the opening in the curtain I'd been peering through then back at me. He shook his head.

"You must be that reporter my deputy told to stay up on the goddamn road."

"He told me to see Chief Deputy Will Black. That's who I'm looking for."

"You found him," he said. "Or, he found you."

"Good. Can I ask you a few questions, Chief Black?"

"Maybe. For now, turn around and put your hands behind your back."

4

THE cuffs had been totally unnecessary. So had the perp walk past the handful of smirking cops still at the scene. The ride into town stuffed into the back seat of a patrol car, hands cuffed behind my back, had been the final straw: Latham County Chief Deputy Will Black moved to the top of my shit list.

When we got to the sheriff's department, located in the basement of the County Courthouse, Will Black stuck me in an interview room. I sat there alone with my thoughts while he checked my press credentials. It was a long check. Two hours later he handed back my press badge and gave me the bare minimum – the who, what, when, and where of the shooting. Then he gave me a thumb toward the door.

When I asked about getting back to my car, he managed a grin. "You'll figure it out."

A deputy ushered me out a side door. From there, it was up the steps and onto the street.

The Latham County Courthouse sat on the south side of the New Bethany town square. Three sides of the square were small shops – a general mercantile, a seed store, a café and the like. On the fourth side was the courthouse, and beside it ran a wide sloping walk leading up to a parking lot – designated parking for courthouse workers and visitors. On the back side of the lot sat a half-dozen patrol cars.

At the front of the lot stood a young woman smiling and waving like she'd been waiting for me all her life.

"You need a ride?" she called and moved hurriedly toward me.

She appeared to be in her early twenties, short and thin but not skinny, with straight blonde hair. She wore slim cut jeans, a floppy white tunic top and carried a purse as big as she was. Her skin was pale as a white horse, her lips a rich carmine red.

I must have appeared confused. Which I was.

"Hey," she said a little breathlessly. "The sheriff's office called me and told me you'd need a ride. I work for the paper, too, so they called me to come get you. You're Gil Coates, aren't you?" She extended her hand.

"Yes." I shook her hand.

"You know, I thought you were older than me, from reading your stories. I. . . oh, sorry, I'm Emily Scott. I just go by Scotts to my friends. And colleagues. Just Scotts."

"Okay, Scotts. Yeah, I need a ride. You know where my car is?"

"I wouldn't be much of a journalist if I didn't. Let's go. I can fill you in on the way."

5

"Sorry about the mess," Scotts said as she climbed into her old orange Jeep. I waited at the door as she reached around, grabbed handfuls of newspapers, magazines, sacks of who-knew-what from the passenger seat and tossed it all into the back.

"Okay, it's safe. Hop in."

She turned the key but the engine struggled to turn over. "Don't worry, it'll start. Travis wants me to get a new car but I say, you know what that would cost? This car is fine. I like it. It goes anywhere, hauls everything. You know what you can do with the money it costs for a new car? You can do a lot, right?"

"Right."

"I mean, Travis – he's my husband – he's a nice man, a *very* nice man. But he worries about me all the time. I told him, look, if the car doesn't start – there, it started, see? Always does. I told him, if the car ever doesn't start, I'll find a phone and call you. No problem."

She whipped the Jeep out of the parking lot, circled the downtown square and headed north.

"So, I know who did it, do you?" she asked, bubbly with excitement.

"Did what?"

"Killed Bobby Rollings, what else?"

"No, I don't. Did you say you worked for the paper?"

"Yeah, I'm a reporter for the *Democrat*, same as you. Well, not exactly the same. I work part-time, whenever they call me. I'm a stringer."

"For Latham County?"

"All around here. Six counties, from Latham, south, all the way to Barstow County."

"A lot of ground to cover."

"My mileage check is bigger than my paycheck. Do you want me to tell you what I know?"

"I do, but slow down for a second." She had the old Jeep hauling it, bounding all over the highway, tires touching down maybe every hundred feet. I wanted to change our pace, see what that cop behind us was doing.

"Sorry. I thought you'd be in a hurry to file your story." She slowed.

"I'm okay," I said.

The cop slowed as we slowed, kept the same distance. So this was my escort out of town, courtesy of Chief Deputy Will Black.

"Okay," I looked back to her, "tell me what you know."

"Everybody around here thinks it was the old man, Jacob Lacobee, who killed him. I mean, this has been brewing for a long time. And it's because of the kid, the little boy. The dead guy – sorry, the victim, Bobby Rollings – you knew his name was Bobby Rollings, didn't you?"

"Yes."

"Bobby Rollings, *Junior,* to be accurate. Anyhow, Bobby Rollings and Jacob Lacobee hated each other. So Rollings, out of spite, they say, decided he wouldn't let Mr. Lacobee see the boy. The boy was Mr. Lacobee's great-grandson, AND, I think this is right, his only male heir. So, he killed Rollings. Or had him killed. Like he always does when he has a problem to solve. Or so they say."

"And you know all this how?"

"I went to church this morning."

"You've lost me."

"I live here, have all my life, and that was all we talked about at church today."

"I see. So, who is Rollings to Jacob Lacobee?"

"Let's see…he would be his…grandson-in-law, I think. Yeah, that sounds right. Jacob Lacobee's granddaughter is the wife of Bobby Rollings. Mother of the boy. Hey, did you see the body?"

"No, I didn't."

"How did you get down here so fast?"

"Drove like a bat out of hell."

She tilted me a grin. "You know what I mean. . .I mean, if you came from Atlanta, that was pretty damn fast. I wonder why they didn't call me?"

"I don't know, but since they didn't – "

"Yeah, yeah I know, 'stick with the program.'"

"Right."

"That's what Travis is always reminding me. I sometimes have a problem with that, though. What is it you think, impatience?"

"I don't know. But look…you live here, you know everyone?"

"Everybody knows everybody *and* their business around here. This isn't Atlanta, you know."

"Sounds like Atlanta to me."

"Except, that's where they live, really."

"Who?"

"Bobby Rollings and his wife. They live in Atlanta. He was some rich guy, worked for a big bank–I can get the name of it if you need it, by the way–and this was, like, their second home. But she grew up here, and…"

She paused for a minute to study a fork in the road then veered left and continued. "Anyhow, she grew up here in New Bethany. I went to school with her, but I was two years behind her so I didn't know her too well. Back then, back in high school, she was a big whore. At least that's what the older girls said. And crazy, too…I almost forgot about that. But that's all just gossip, you know. For what that's worth."

My experience had been that gossip was worth quite a bit. It spoke to possibilities, and while seldom the drop-dead truth, it could point you in the right direction.

"You went to school with Mrs. Rollings? I saw her this morning, she looks older."

Scotts was pleased by the idea. "How old do you think I am? How about I have a daughter fourteen years old this year? Figure it out. Of course, I did start young."

"I would have guessed twenty something."

"Gee, thanks. Lorelei! That's it, Lorelei!" she said abruptly.

"What?"

"Brain freeze. Couldn't think of it for a second, but that's her name, Lorelei Rollings. It was Lacobee back then. Her dad got killed in Vietnam – then her mother ran off and joined some hippie commune. She was mostly raised by her grandparents. That's the Lacobees, her daddy's parents. They're rich as coots, you know, own about half of Latham County. They supposedly own the biggest plantation in Georgia. That's what they say. I can find that out for sure for you, if you need it."

She slowed the car as the road narrowed. I glanced back to see the trailing cop was no longer there. We were close to the road that led down to the Rollings home. As she made the corner, I saw my car sitting on the shoulder. The road was otherwise empty, nothing in the cul-de-sac down around the Rollings place, no cars in the drive. The entire little hollow was still and silent.

"That your car?" she asked, suddenly a little gloomy looking.

"That's it. Pull in behind for a minute, I need to ask you a few more questions."

"Sure thing." She perked back up. She wheeled in, slammed the Jeep to a stop and turned to face me. "What's the question?"

"You said the sheriff's office called you to pick me up. Who called, and what did they say?"

She screwed her mouth quizzically, like I'd presented a real puzzler. "Hmmm. Wow. So you can make something out of that?"

"I want to be clear. Who called you, and what did they say?"

"Yeah, sure, okay. So, the Sheriff's office called – it was the dispatcher, Boyd O'Con – I'm sure about that because he's my cousin. So, Boyd – he's just a part-timer, it's not a real big police force you know – he called and said that you – and he used your name, Gil Coates from the *Democrat*, I'm sure he said that – he said that you would need a ride to your car from the sheriff's office. He asked if I could pick you up and take you to it. That's it. That's all. He didn't say why you were there or how long you'd been there. I told him yes, and he told me to be in the parking lot outside the west exit at two o'clock. There I was, there you were, right on time."

"When did he call you?"

"About one o'clock."

"And you never talked to the Chief Deputy, Will Black?"

"Not today. But, I've talked to him before. I mean I know him, you know. I've been working for the paper almost three years, so I'm in there a lot. He's okay. No kidding, he is. He looks rattlesnake mad all the time, and his people skills aren't the best, but he's okay. My dad knows him. They're friends. He says he's okay, so he is."

"That wasn't my experience," I said.

I took a minute to consider what more to ask of her. Calvin Daniels had said to keep it mum, but a local insider could be helpful. I decided to give her some simple follow up and ask Mr. Manship about using her on the story.

"I've got to get back to Atlanta, but I need you to do two things for me. Give me your number, I'll call you tomorrow."

"Sure," she said, grabbing her purse, pulling out a pad and pencil. "What do you need?"

At that moment we heard a car coming up from behind. A Latham County Sheriff's car. The driver looked like the same one who'd tailed us out of town. The car crawled past, did a slow turn around in the cul-de-sac in front of the Rollings house, then pulled up and stopped beside us.

It was the deputy from earlier, Weaver. He let his mirrored aviator sunglasses stare at us a moment, then peeled them off and rolled down his window. "Still a crime scene down there, so stay away."

"Yes, John, we know," Scotts sighed impatiently. "We're just getting his car, if you don't mind."

"No, I don't mind," he said and pulled his glasses back on. "You need to be moving on, that's all."

"Right, John, we are, we are."

He allowed his sunglasses to give us a final warning glare and then pulled away.

"He is *such* an uptight jerk," she said.

"You know him?"

"Twelve years of school together, and he's a complete gizmo from day one! Anyhow, what else do you need?"

"Find out from your cop cousin who had him call you to pick me up. Then let him talk. Make notes on every word. Oh, and check the blotter, too. I didn't have a chance, your Chief gave me the bum's rush."

"Did that already," Scotts said. "The call came in at 6:05 this morning. It was Lorelei Rollings. According to the log, she was quote, hysterical, unquote. And she said, quote, My grandfather killed my husband, unquote."

"That's good," I said with an appreciative nod. "And interesting. Maybe your congregation knows what they're talking about."

She lifted one side of her mouth in a half grin. "Sometimes the church people get it right. What else?"

"This might be trickier – see if you can find out who was delivering the local newspaper out here this morning. It was a gray van, carrier number 1515 for the *New Bethany Banner*. Get a name, see if you can talk to him and find out why was he talking to the cops this morning, what he told them. Keep it under the radar. Let's not let the cops know we know about this guy. Can you do that?"

She formed a big smile as she wrote down her telephone number and handed it to me.

"Yes, I can."

I hopped out. She roared off.

6

I had a couple of hours before I needed to head back to Atlanta, so I spent the time familiarizing myself with Latham County.

I drove back into New Bethany to learn my way around. That didn't take long. At the downtown diner, I grabbed a burger and listened to the waitress speculate on who had killed Bobby Rollings that morning and why. A reporter from a competitor, *The Atlanta Constitution,* drifted into the diner as I was finishing and told me he was being stonewalled by the local cops. I acted surprised to hear that.

A little later, the fellow who ran the Citgo station – the only service station in town open on Sunday – told me what he knew about Jacob Lacobee. He confirmed what Scotts had said earlier: Lacobee was the big dog in these parts.

"He's not the fella you want to get in a bare-knuckle fight with," the Citgo man said. "He'd be using more'n his fists."

He gave me directions to the Lacobee place, which he said was listed on some historic register as Montrose Plantation. I drove out to see it. I noted it was only a few miles south of the Rollings place.

There was no activity anywhere on or around the plantation that I could see. That seemed odd given all that had happened that day. But that was the story almost everywhere I went. By all appearances, today was like any other Easter Sunday in the sunny South

– quiet and peaceful, serene in the breezes of spring and a new life cycle.

Either that or the killing of Bobby Rollings, Jr., had scared the town so much they'd all decided to stay inside.

7

O<small>N</small> the drive back to Atlanta, I pulled out my micro-cassette recorder and dictated notes. I filled both sides of the tape. It had been an eventful day.

As I approached the lights of the city, my thoughts turned to the call I was to make to Mr. Manship. While I didn't do *anxiety* – or if I did, it was never more than the low-grade variety – I couldn't help wonder what this meeting was about.

Adam Manship wasn't just the owner and publisher of *The Atlanta Democrat.* It was his flagship paper, but he owned a dozen more daily metros across the South. He also owned as many television stations, three billboard companies along the east coast, two or three radio networks out west and a Madison Avenue ad agency. He was, to put it in the parlance of the day, a media mogul. He was a big deal.

What was it about this story, this small-town murder, that caught his attention? What had prompted him to pull a reporter – something he had apparently never done – order complete secrecy, block printing the story, and ask for a personal report?

And why me? Was this some kind of reprimand? My last shot? Calvin Daniels was right, I *had* been an asshole around the paper after they killed the Makar story – a story I'd spent over a year on. I knew I was on thin ice with my immediate boss, City Editor Paul

Christie. Maybe I had been expressing my frustration a little too loudly, a little too often. Maybe I was about to be sent packing.

The questions and the second guessing kept whirling through my mind. By the time I got back to Atlanta and to a phone, I'd found I *did* do anxiety after all.

8

M<small>Y</small> phone call was answered by a formal-sounding woman who told me to come to Mr. Manship's residence – the penthouse atop the Chesterfield Towers in downtown Atlanta – at 9 p.m.

I was there promptly at nine, in my suit and tie, and was welcomed in by the woman I'd spoken to on the phone. She introduced herself as Mrs. Christian and said Mr. Manship would see me right away. She offered a tiny nod and told me to follow her please. On the way down a long corridor, she asked if I'd like anything to drink – coffee, tea, a beer perhaps? I declined.

She opened the door to an expansive study with a floor-to-ceiling window that ran the entire width of the building. The lighting throughout the room was dim and indirect, allowing a clear and sparkling panorama of the Atlanta skyline. It was an impressive view.

I recognized Mr. Manship sitting across the room in a thick leather club chair, a soft-lit lamp on the table beside him. He wore tan trousers, a loose fitting white shirt and was making notes on a pad in his lap while smoking a cigar. From a vent in the ceiling directly above him came a soft whirring sound, drawing the cigar smoke in a spiral up and out of the room.

"Mr. Manship," Mrs. Christian called across the room to him, "Mr. Coates is here."

He looked up and around, eyes searching through the shadows. "Oh, good," he said and stood up. "Come over, please, and have a seat."

We shook hands, exchanged formal greetings and a pleasantry or two, and after declining another offer of a drink – a Scotch this time – I took a seat in the leather chair opposite his.

He looked to my escort and with a gentle nod said, "Thank you, Mrs. Christian, that's all for now."

She dismissed herself.

"A very good Puerto Rican cigar," he said as he gazed at the perfect ash on the tip of the one he held. "Are you sure you wouldn't like one?"

"No thank you, sir."

He smiled slightly. "Much like one I purchased some years ago. I remember the maker, an old fellow at a quaint little cigar shop tucked away on the shady Calle San Francisco in old San Juan. Not far from the Cathedral San Juan de Bautista and the hotel El Convento, where Sarah and I always lodged. On Sunday mornings, we'd sit on the terrace overlooking the cathedral, enjoying strong coffee and pastries, being serenaded by a grand choir and a priest with a genuinely lovely tenor singing high mass in Latin. That was December, many years ago. It was warm there but pleasant enough in the mornings with the breeze off the ocean. The waters glistened a deep aquamarine. . . But, that was then."

"Sounds like an important *then*, sir," I said.

He smiled, again, slightly, "It was, yes. It was."

Mr. Manship wasn't an old man at the time. He was in his early sixties, but he seemed to carry more years than that in the lines of his face, his weary eyes. He had an almost bald head, a pale, damp complexion and was short and stout in build. Some might have called him portly. He had that liquid tremor of the eye that seemed to suggest some deep emotion running through his heart.

He glanced down at the note pad he'd held in his lap, then set it on the table and looked at me. "What's the story on the Rollings murder?"

9

I opened my notes and told him what I knew. He listened intently, never stopping me to question anything. He did offer a brief smile at my detention by Chief Deputy Black, and again at being picked up by the paper's stringer, Emily Scott. Otherwise, he sat poker-faced and silent, absorbed yet oddly distant.

"It's not much of a story so far," I concluded.

He considered what I'd said. "No, not so far. But, I wonder... who kills someone on Easter Sunday?"

"That *is* curious."

"Yes, it is. And you say it occurred at dawn?"

"Right at daybreak, from what I could gather."

"I wonder what *that* means?" he said mostly to himself and folded his hands across his lap.

As he sat there, ruminating, I considered what to add, what to ask, what to do next. I didn't have to consider long.

"That was exceptional work on the Makar story, Mr. Coates. Exceptional. Good old-fashioned digging and bull-dogging. Maybe even a little bullying, too, eh?"

He pointed his cigar at me with a smile, then drew a puff. "Weren't you a Marine?"

"Yes, sir."

"Combat correspondent, wasn't it?"

"Yes, sir. For a year. I was part of the team covering Operation Frequent Wind – last days of the Vietnam conflict."

"Some conflict." He looked off for a moment with a dark gaze, then turned back. "So, you're a leatherneck – stout of heart and tough of mind, as they say. Resourceful, too, it seems, with friends in high places."

He smiled again and tamped out his cigar. "Very good, very good. What we need."

He took a deep breath and clamped his hands on the arms of his chair.

"In any case, I'm sorry we had to hold your Makar story. There were reasons. Compelling ones – at least for me. I understand you've been quite put out with us about that, and I don't blame you. One day, perhaps, I can explain. I'd like to be able to do that."

He rose and stood for a moment, as if securing his stance, then slowly proceeded across the room to a distant wall. The room was not only expansive, but richly appointed. There were paintings hung in almost every available space. One was signed "Monet," another signed "Cezanne." There were sculptures on pedestals here and there, and a grouping of stunning black and white photographs. One entire wall was floor-to-ceiling mahogany shelves filled with leather-bound books.

This world of his was saturated in works of art and literature.

He stopped across the way, pulled a painting off the wall and opened a wall safe behind it. He removed an envelope, then closed it and shuffled back to his chair.

"I want you to fly to D.C. tomorrow morning and meet a friend of ours. His name is Gary Hooper. He's a *Wall Street Journal* reporter. He knows what to talk to you about. He'll meet you at the D.C. airport. I'll have someone pick you up at 6 a.m. and take you to the plane. Pack for a night or two, that will do. Can you be ready?"

"Yes, sir, I can."

He looked at me a long moment.

"You would be the odd fellow if you didn't wonder about all this, Mr. Coates. But I don't want to tell you too much, it'd ruin it for you. I will tell you that I am trying to solve a puzzle – a puzzle nature has not posed."

I nodded.

"I need this story to do that. I'm enlisting your help. I will require the strictest of confidence from you. I'll speak to your bosses at the paper, get you cleared so all you will do for now is report to me. Clear so far?"

"Yes, sir, clear."

"Fine. Now here's ten thousand dollars in cash." He handed me the envelope he'd taken from the safe. "Use it as you need to. Trust me, you will need to."

He looked at me with a trace of a smile. "Any questions?"

It did occur to me at the moment, bewildered as I was, that I should ask about the stringer I'd gotten involved. That had been a mistake, I now saw. I would need to back her out immediately.

Before I could say anything Mr. Manship added, "The stringer you mentioned, the young lady – it sounds like she might be helpful to you. Put her to work as you see fit. She already works for us, so she's been vetted. Just be sure she understands the level of confidentiality I require."

"I will, yes, sir. And if I could, one question."

"Sure."

"Do I still work for *The Democrat*? Use my press credentials, contacts and the like?"

He smiled. "Yes you do, of course. I can see the confusion, but your status hasn't changed. The only difference is now you file your story with me, not the paper. I'm your one and only reader."

"I understand, sir."

"Only partly," he said, an amused twinkle in his eye. "But we'll get you there before it's over."

He told me to call when I returned from Washington then had Mrs. Christian show me out.

10

SIDEBAR:
"The Arts Need More Than Your Applause"

Excerpt: *ATLANTA TODAY MAGAZINE*
September Issue, 1987

Adam Manship rarely grants interviews, except when it comes to the aid of his passion: The arts and artists. That's why he agreed to talk with us about the upcoming *Exhibition Internationale*, which opens next month at the Eloise Tipton Museum of Art in downtown Atlanta.

Manship, owner/publisher of *The Atlanta Democrat* and dozens more media properties across the country, will have fourteen works of art on loan for the exhibit. He will also be donating a painting from his collection for auction at the Tipton's annual fundraiser the same month. As one of the country's best known art lovers, Manship's collection is well documented and his purchases are highly anticipated and publicized. He is known in the international art world as one of a very few "branded collectors."

When a branded collector makes a purchase, especially of a work by an unknown artist, it can make the young artist a star overnight. That's exactly what has happened to one young Canadian artist whose works will be included in the show.

"There will be four new works by Susan Clarry in the *Exhibition Internationale*," Manship said. "She has a unique, contemporary vision and an originality and daring we rarely see in one so young. We anticipate she will become a major voice in contemporary art and stay there for a long time."

Manship has always been generous in lending parts of his collection to museums and exhibitions, usually on the condition that the show include the works of one or more new, unknown artists.

He does more than just purchase art by new artists. Much as art patrons of the Renaissance did, he will often offer a stipend to a young artist in return for first rights on future works.

Any time an auction house or museum curator describes a work as "Collected by Manship" or "Owned by Manship," it tends to push the price of the artist's work up considerably.

That's exactly what curators at the Tipton are hoping for next month. Not only will they be exhibiting new works by Ms. Clarry, they'll be auctioning one of her paintings during their annual museum fundraiser, compliments of Adam Manship.

11

THE passenger manifest for the Monday morning flight to Washington D.C. consisted of one – me. A pilot and co-pilot manned the cockpit and were in the final phase of running their pre-flight as I stepped aboard. The co-pilot waved me inside, showed me where to stow my bag and offered a cup of coffee. With a small gesture toward the empty cabin he said, "Good thing you got here early, you wouldn't have gotten a seat."

I hoped he was a better pilot than comedian.

The Manship plane was a Dassault Falcon 900 which originally seated about twenty but had been converted to executive comfort and luxury for a half dozen passengers. The row seating had been replaced by a wide leather chairs that swiveled, reclined and probably gave you a warm massage if you wanted. I settled in for the finest plane ride I'd ever had.

There were recent issues of the *Wall Street Journal* in a rack near the back of the cabin. I thumbed through a few and saw that the man I would be meeting, Gary Hooper, covered the Department of Justice. His stories – there were three in the half-dozen papers I scanned – focused on a DOJ investigation of securities violations by two Wall Street investment firms. A sidebar noted a parallel investigation into fraud by an unnamed banking firm.

I wondered if that had anything to do with the meeting Manship had arranged for me. Or with the Rollings murder. Rollings had been, according to Scotts, some kind of hot-shot banker. And the *Journal* stories I'd just read had been no more than a week old. Maybe there was a connection.

Last night's meeting with Mr. Manship had been a new kind of experience for me. I was no surer where I stood after the meeting than I was going in. And yet I was oddly reassured. Perhaps it had been what he'd said: "I'm trying to solve a puzzle nature has not posed." I liked that. It seemed to suggest that, for him anyway, ambiguity and certainty could peacefully co-exist. It seemed to suggest for me, in that he was enlisting my help, that I hadn't been demoted and exiled to the boonies. At least not yet.

12

GARY Hooper was waiting on the tarmac when I got off the plane in D.C. He was an enormous man, standing about six feet six, weighing at least 275 pounds without an ounce of fat. His shoulders were the width of a pickup truck. He looked to be fifteen years my senior and had a hint of gray in his close cut hair. He wore a light gray suit and a welcoming smile.

We shook hands and he steered us toward a small, well-lit building attached to the hangars for private planes. It was a diner for execs and their pilots.

We ordered breakfast, drew a cup of coffee from the urn and took a table. He put his cup down, reached into his jacket pocket and pulled out a thick envelope. He slid it across the table.

"If I know Mr. Manship, he didn't tell you much."

"Nothing but your name."

"That's his way, close to the vest. Don't take it personally. I've known him twenty years. Gave me my first newspaper job. Twenty years later, I still can't figure him. All I'm sure of is he counts on me and I can count on him."

"I gather that."

"He must think he can count on you. Otherwise, we wouldn't be here."

"I talked to him privately for the first time last night. Had no idea he knew me or anything about me."

"What he knows will surprise you," he said, looking up from his coffee. His words seemed without shadowy intent, more just matter of fact.

After a moment, he glanced at his watch. "I have a meeting and it could be a long one. I may not get back with you until tomorrow. I want to introduce you to my guy at DOJ. Meanwhile, read that."

He pointed to the envelope he'd given me. "Copies of my notes and summaries of a DOJ investigation. Nothing you could print at this point, but it involves your dead guy. Read them, then burn them."

He stood up, looked around, then turned back to me. "Here's your hotel info. I'll call you there. Taxis are right out that door."

He was gone.

13

"**M**URDERED Banker Stole $6 Million from Nuns."
That would have been my headline based on Hooper's notes.

Much of the information was, as he'd said, still unusable – it was either highly circumstantial or uncorroborated. It came from several different DOJ investigations at various stages of completion. But there was some compelling financial evidence piling up.

Hooper must have had a good source inside Justice because his notes weren't just about Bobby Rollings – an investment banker who had clearly bilked a Catholic Order of Nuns out of $6 million dollars. They described a web of looting and larceny that involved a major bank and over $50 billion in trust funds.

That part of the investigation was of special interest to me because it focused on a familiar bank – the one our paychecks were drawn on. Coincidentally, the one Bobby Rollings worked for.

All of which begged the age-old investigator's question: When is a coincidence not a coincidence?

By the end of the day, I'd gone through Hooper's notes several times and made notes of my own. I made a list of questions I wanted to ask him.

Done with his notes, I stepped onto my balcony and smoked three cigarettes while I burned them. It felt like an awful lot of intrigue to me – the notes didn't seem to rise to the standard of *state secrets* or anything – but I almost always do what I'm told. Unless I see a reason not to.

Hooper called mid-afternoon to say he would be tied up the rest of the day and to plan a breakfast meeting tomorrow at my hotel. He suggested a restaurant for me to try for dinner and gave me the number of the car service to use. He recommended I not go strolling through the streets of D.C. after dark.

Before going to dinner, I called Scotts to check on her progress. Since Mr. Manship had given his okay, I loaded her up with spade work. I also told her that from this minute forward our investigation was on the QT, her only contact would be me, and nothing she learned, *absolutely nothing,* was to be discussed with anyone else. Nothing. Never. Nobody.

"Okay, okay, I get it!" she'd said.

"I want to be sure you understand."

"I do, I do. I mean, I don't, but I do. Okay, so get this… my editor called this morning first thing – oh, I meant to ask if you know him, Charles Norman? He works the state desk, and I'm pretty sure he only handles the stringers?"

"I know him."

"So Mr. Norman calls first thing this morning and tells me the paper isn't covering this story at all and for me to stay away from it."

"Okay."

"That's what he said, 'Stay away.' He was emphatic about it. Like you are about keeping it quiet."

"And I'm telling you that you and I *are* working it, and I have more for you to do. But, we're off the books. The *why* doesn't matter."

"Well, now…okay, but…" She hemmed and hawed. "How do I get paid if I can't turn in a story? I mean, that's how they pay me –

by the story – and I really do need the money, or I'll have to get a job. I mean a full-time paying job."

"I'll pay you, direct, in cash. No records, just cash every week. Three hundred a week. How's that?"

She laughed so loud I had to push the phone from my ear.

"How does a girl say no to that?" she said. "I'm in! What else do you need?"

"Anything on the guy delivering papers?"

"Not yet. Everybody's all hush-hush down here. I think it's as much confusion as secrecy, though. We don't get a lot of murders."

"Could be," I said. "Look, we also need everything you can get on the banks there in Latham County. Total assets, board members, full workup."

"Done. But…hey, why do you think this has something to do with the banks?"

I told her what my first editor told me: "Look, listen, don't ask why."

14

THE next morning, Hooper called and changed the plans. We would be skipping the breakfast meeting and heading to the airport shortly after noon. He'd be at the hotel by two at the latest.

I spent the morning on the phone with our research department in Atlanta. I asked them to pull everything they had on Jacob Lacobee of New Bethany, Georgia, and get it to me pronto.

It was quite the file.

Lacobee was 71 years old, born in 1917 on the family spread, Montrose. The place was already a large, successful cotton plantation. When he took over operation from his father in the mid-forties, he expanded the property by buying out neighboring farms. Today, the place had over 18,000 acres in production and at peak season employed several hundred hands.

Lacobee held a lot of sway, locally and statewide. He was a major contributor to every politician within reach and hosted annual dove hunts that included the Who's Who of Georgia politics and commerce. He owned the two largest cotton gins in the state, the Latham County farmer's coop, and was a board member and stockholder of two banks, the most notable being Georgia Commerce Bank.

Notable for being the one Rollings worked for and the one mentioned in the DOJ investigation.

He was married to Eva (nee Talley) Lacobee, who had brought a dowry of financial wealth and over 3,000 acres of adjacent farmland to the union. They had had one son, Joseph, who had been killed in a car wreck, one granddaughter, Lorelei Lacobee Rollings, and one great-grandson.

Scotts had been right: The boy, Robert Rollings, III, was Lacobee's only living male heir.

Gary Hooper missed his mark by a few hours – he didn't pick me up at my hotel until rush-hour. I thought Atlanta had the world's worst traffic but I was wrong. It was D.C. We could have walked to the airport faster.

"You happen to read the story on Edgar Meadows," Hooper said, tapping the *Journal* he'd laid in the seat when we got into the airport limo.

"No, but I will," I said. I didn't want to tell him I had only the vaguest idea who Edgar Meadows was.

The story informed me. Meadows was the governor of Arizona, and he'd just been convicted, in an impeachment trial, on charges of obstruction of justice and misuse of public funds. He was to be removed from office tomorrow.

"That's where I'm headed," Hooper said as our driver pulled into the airport. "Arizona. Ever been?"

"I haven't."

"Today's agenda is this: We're taking you back to Atlanta – probably get there by ten tonight – then I'm on my way to Arizona and a meeting with Governor Meadows."

"Does this have anything to do with the story you're on?"

"No idea."

"Really?"

"Really."

"Is this your life? Crisscrossing the country?"

"I go where the boss sends me."

"Why's the *Journal* sending you to Meadows?"

"They're not. I'm at the pleasure of Mr. Manship now."

He turned away, as if to say we had nothing more to discuss.

We took our seats on the Manship plane and were airborne in minutes. Hooper had been fumbling with papers in his briefcase and after a short time clicked the case shut and looked at me.

"Did you burn the notes?"

"Burned and flushed," I said.

I'd already decided to scratch all the small questions I'd jotted down for him. There was a larger one to ask.

"I could have gotten all this information any number of ways, most of them faster and simpler than this. What's the deal?"

He smiled and considered it for a moment as he looked out the window. "I was going to take you to meet my source today. He's with DOJ, might have been able to tell you more on your dead guy."

We felt the plane take a smooth bank turn then level out and gun it. "Headed south now," he said almost to himself. "See how orange those wings get in that western sun?"

I looked at the wings. They were orange. So what?

"I came to D.C. to get this part of the story from you?" I asked.

He looked at me then turned back toward the window. "No idea." After a moment, he added, "Did you know that Mr. Manship is on the board of Georgia Commerce Bank?"

"I expected he would be. It's the bank the paper uses."

"It's also the bank the DOJ is investigating," he said.

"And Rollings worked for," I said.

"Right."

"All that was in your notes. I figure the bank had to be part of the initial investigation for them to find that business on Rollings and the nuns. That the way it happened?"

I was guessing. And fishing.

"Probably.   But in the course of investigating the bank, and then Rollings, they found something else. Something else NOT Rollings, NOT the bank. Something else."

"But you don't know what that something else is."

"Only that it's local. I don't think DOJ knows what they've got at this point."

"This unknown, then, could that be the connection to the Rollings murder?"

"It probably wasn't the nuns," he said with a big grin. Then he returned his gaze out the window, to the orange wings.

"I see," I said to him.

But I didn't.

15

"MEADOWS and Mr. Manship are thick as thieves," Hooper said casually, as the plane started its descent into Fulton County Airport. "Meadows owned two dozen newspapers at one time, back before he was elected Governor of Arizona. He and Manship go way back. I think, but I'm not sure, that Meadows helped Manship buy his first newspaper thirty-some years ago. I imagine they did a lot of drinking together over the years, while they sat around fixing ad rates, busting unions."

He grinned and added, "God knows what else. Made some enemies I'll bet."

"And those ink stains last longer than blood stains," I said.

"Yes they do," he said.

We felt the plane touch down. The pilot had told us when we boarded that he would only be on the ground in Atlanta long enough for me to get off and for him to refuel the plane. Then they'd be on the way to Arizona.

"I appreciate your help, Gary," I said as I grabbed my one small bag. "I hope I get the chance to work with you more."

"Unlikely any time soon. The *Journal* is sending me to the Middle East – Kuwait to be precise – to open a bureau there. Leave next week, I think. Big raise, big expense account, big desert."

"Kuwait? Damn, what's there?"

"Don't know. The boys upstairs must know something. We'll see."

"You go where they send you."

"That's what I do."

"Safe travels, then."

16

SIDEBAR:
"Meadows Impeached: A First for Arizona"

Excerpt: *The Arizona Sun Ledger, April 5, 1988*

PHOENIX, Az. – The Arizona State Senate voted today to remove first-term Governor Edgar Meadows from office effective immediately. The impeachment trial and vote was the first ever for the State of Arizona and followed months of hearings and criminal investigations.

Because Arizona has no Lieutenant Governor, Speaker of the House Taylor Burford will become governor pending a special election.

The Senate voted 26 to 4 to convict Meadows of obstruction of justice in connection with an FBI investigation into his administration's misuse of public funds. The Senate also voted 21-9 to convict him of multiple violations of campaign finance laws. Meadows may still face criminal charges in each of the cases.

The vote to impeach was 24 in favor, 5 against, and one abstention.

A separate vote to disqualify Meadows from ever holding state office again failed to get the two-thirds majority required.

Meadows later told reporters that he would be returning to public office.

"I will be back, you can count on that," he said.

Meadows was in the second year of his first term as governor. Prior to winning the state's top job, he had served two terms as a state senator.

Before his entry into Arizona politics, Meadows owned some twenty newspapers across the Southwest, including major publications in Arizona, New Mexico and Nevada. His publications were a dominant voice in politics in all three states.

As required by state law, he sold his media properties when he became governor. The sale was to Manship Media Corporation.

Meadows' move to divest himself of media holdings was openly criticized at the time by political opponents. They claimed the divestiture was "a shoddy sham, a temporary, paper-only transfer to an old friend." They pointed to his longstanding partnerships with media mogul Adam Manship, whose company purchased all of the Meadows publications.

"We don't believe for a minute that the Governor is not still pulling the strings at those newspapers," said State Senator Carlos Barbosa, a Republican from Tucson. "The people of Arizona deserve better than this con artist."

17

THE airport limo got me to my apartment shortly after midnight. The street was silent, the sky inky and starless. As I started inside I saw a cop car moving slowly down the street. That was unusual for our quiet neighborhood. All the more unusual because it was a Latham County Sheriff's car, not an Atlanta city cop.

As he passed under the streetlight I recognized the guy: it was Weaver, the tight-ass deputy from the crime scene. He kept eyes forward like he wasn't looking, but I'm sure he saw me.

I made a note to ask Chief Deputy Will Black what his boys were doing on the prowl in Atlanta, in front of my apartment, at midnight. Wasn't that about seventy-five miles outside their jurisdiction?

When I opened the door to my place, I was ready for a long night's sleep, but I was hoping for a quick bunk-up with Lacey Moore first. All that remained of Lacey was a cryptic note:

> "Not waiting any longer, asshole. Gone home. Your new friend, Scotty, or some namey-poo like that — what is she, a goddamn pet? – called here five times before 11 p.m! She must be in heat. I was, now I'm not."

> —Your Long Gone Snatch

It was true I hadn't called Lacey in two days, but this seemed an overreaction. I shouldn't have been surprised. She could be a drama queen. That made her a damn good litigator for the DA's office but at times a difficult playmate.

Neither of us began the relationship thinking we were going anywhere together except to bed and maybe thru career doors we'd open for one another. We had a tacit *quid pro quo:* She got frequent publicity, I got inside info. But in truth, I was getting accustomed to her being around. I liked it. I liked *her* – she could be, and often was, a kind, thoughtful, understanding woman. Just not tonight.

I fell into the chair at my desk and turned on the IBM Selectric. It was part of my routine to transfer hand-written and recorded notes to typed notes; it helped clarify the details of the day. With no Lacey to play with, I might as well.

But I couldn't get started: Too many notes, too many thoughts of Lacey.

I stared in the mirror across from the desk and studied the scar that ran just above my eyebrow. For some quirky reason, Lacey loved to rub it, gently, soothingly; to pull her fingers through my hair and whisper in a curious voice, always as if for the first time, "Tell me how you got this."

I would tell her a different story every time she asked. It was usually a story I'd make up on the spot, though sometimes it'd be a story I'd fashioned beforehand, had ready for her.

She called them my Arabian Nights Tales, and in some way they were. Tales to give me another night with her, to buy more time. In case she *was* the one.

One day I would tell her about the scar. I might have this night, if she'd been there.

But it was too late to call her now. And too late to call Scotts – who I would explain to Lacey as my new assistant, assigned to me by the paper for this one story only. Which was mostly true.

Instead of trying to figure out what two women wanted, I clicked off the typewriter, had two beers and a cigarette, and fell into an empty sack.

18

M Y phone rang early the next morning.
"Got something for you! Are you ready for this? Who is on the board of the bank Bobby Rollings worked for? And who do we have an interview with? Guess. They're one and the same. Guess!"

Scotts, apparently, was not one to identify herself on the phone. She was one to talk and presume the content of the call would reveal the caller.

"This better be good, it's six a.m."

"Lacobee! Jacob Lacobee! The dead guy's grandfather-in-law. He's the one everyone thinks killed Bobby Rollings?"

"So you say."

"So we go ask him. I called him, asked if we could do a feature story for the paper on his family's loss, and you know what he said?"

"No."

"'Not much of a loss.'"

"Is that so?"

"He said, quote: *Not much of a loss.*"

"Interesting."

"It's ballsy!" she said.

"Is that what you'd call it?"

"It is when you say it to a newspaper three days after the poor guy is blown to smithereens? Yeah, I'd call it that. What should I call it?"

"Close enough. What time is the interview?"

"He said we could come anytime, he was always there."

"Meet me at the Sheriff's Office at noon. I've got some questions for Will Black first, we'll go from there."

Before heading to Latham County, I made a stop at the paper to check messages and to see what kind of coverage the competition was giving the Rollings killing. While Manship had blocked the story across all his outlets, our competitors were playing it up big. Our cross-town rival ran with a juicy, bloodthirsty headline: "Banker Dead in Easter Sunday Shotgun Slaying."

Not bad, not bad at all.

The Latham County paper, *The New Bethany Banner*, went with the tell-it-all-at-once headline, "Atlanta Banker Found Murdered At His Latham County Home On Easter Sunday Morning." This is the story that followed:

> NEW BETHANY, Ga. – Latham County Sheriff's Deputies have found no apparent motive and only a few leads in the Easter Sunday morning murder of an Atlanta investment banker.
>
> Robert Rollings, Jr., 37, was found lying on the back lawn of his Latham County residence by his wife shortly after sunrise on Sunday morning, dead of multiple gunshot wounds, according to Latham County Chief Deputy Will Black.
>
> Rollings was killed by a double shotgun blast at close range, according to Latham County coroner Dr. Archie Cook. "I would say the range was about five feet or closer," said Cook. "The wadding from the shot hit the body."
>
> One blast of Number One buckshot hit Rollings in the face and a second shot entered his body approximately four inches below his right shoulder, penetrating his heart and lungs, the coroner said.

Two of the buckshot exited on the left side of the body. "He was probably dead before he hit the ground," the coroner said.

The coroner placed the time of death at approximately 6 a.m. The weapon used in the murder was identified as a probable 12-guage shotgun, according to sheriff's deputies. No weapon has been found at this time, they said.

The victim's wife, Lorelei Rollings, called the Latham County Sheriff's Office shortly after 6 a.m. and reported that she had found her husband shot outside their home, according to deputies. The victim had a young son, Robert Rollings, III, 5, and he reportedly was home at the time of the shooting.

According to deputies, robbery was not the motive. "He still had his ring and watch on and nothing seems to have been taken from his cars or around the house," said Black.

The Sheriff's Office is in the process of investigating the murder.

Before leaving Atlanta, I called Mr. Manship's number as instructed. Mrs. Christian told me he would see me that evening at 9 p.m., if that was convenient for me. That was convenient, I told her.

I also tried to call Lacey but it was apparently *not* convenient for her to talk to me – despite the fact that she was sitting right there in her office, alone, drinking coffee and staring out the window, according to her paralegal, Myrna. I left the message that I'd call her another time – some time when her panties weren't in a wad. The snickering Myrna said she'd tell her that.

It was still early, and the weather was cool and sunny, so I decided to take the bike to Latham County. I hadn't ridden my Triumph Bonneville in almost four months – the winter had been harsh and

I'd become a fair-weather rider. I needed to work the rust off both me and the bike on some back roads, and old Highway 37 had enough twists and turns to do just that. The traffic would be light once I got out of Atlanta, so I could open her up, blow out the system and get there in plenty of time.

I shoved my pocket recorder, pad and pen into my jacket and took off.

I was rolling into Latham County before I knew it. Just past the county line, I had to downshift quickly and slow to a crawl. Dead ahead, surrounding the Flint River Bridge like the old bridge was a fleeing felon, were a dozen cop cars. As I got closer, I saw two empty boat trailers. Down below, in the waters just out from the bridge, two boats were dragging lines in an ever-widening spiral. Inside one boat were scuba divers, suited up, ready to jump in.

Chief Deputy Will Black was standing alone and solemn on the shoulder of the road, scratching his chin and alternating glances between the boats and me.

"You got a jumper?" I called to him as I killed the engine and dismounted.

"No comment," he said and turned away with a sharp pivot.

I walked up beside him and stood quietly. I watched the boats below and saw they weren't pulling hooks, they were dragging nets. No jumper here, these guys were looking for some *thing*.

I leaned in to him. "I was on my way to your office to get the latest on the Rollings case. Looks like the latest is we have an idea where the murder weapon is."

He looked at me and sniffed, then turned back toward the boats and started talking.

"Off the record, we got lucky. Witness saw a car stop on the bridge Sunday morning, throw something in the water, then haul ass. Witness was down there," he pointed to a boat launch, "taking a piss."

"Damn."

"Like I said, lucky."

"So, he must have seen the car, too?"

He gave me a smart-ass grin. "Man, you're some sharp cookie!" He paused then went on. "Off the record, a yellow Cadillac, he thinks. Older model."

"That helps?"

"It does."

"And yet, you don't seem all that excited."

"It's a long way between here and an arrest." He turned to face me squarely. "But I don't need to tell you all this, do I? This ain't your first rodeo. So don't give me that naive horseshit."

"And I thought we had such a special connection."

He studied me. "I'll give you a special connection, since you're looking. First, nothing about this case is going to be pretty, and for a lot of us it ain't going to be easy, either. Most of us are pretty goddamn sure where it's headed and we are not looking forward to it. You follow?"

"I do. Is there more?"

"Yeah, there's more, wise guy. And I don't like it, but I'm gonna do it anyhow."

"What's that?"

"Keep an eye on your sorry ass while you're down here because I get the feeling you're going to get it in a lot of trouble. You and that girl, Buddy Adams' daughter."

"Emily Scott?"

"The both of you. Big pile of shit if you don't watch it. Don't be mistaken about that."

"But, you're going to watch our backs."

"That's what I said. And you know why?"

"It's not because you like us."

"Correct. Because I hate all the goddamn paperwork that goes with finding dead bodies."

"Is that a threat?"

"Hell no, that's no threat. It's a caution. A goddamn serious one."

"Is that why you've got your boys tailing me? To keep an eye on me? That one last night right outside my place. . . I don't like that kind of shit."

"Got no idea what you're talking about."

"Yes you do."

He gave me a cold, hard stare.

"You have your boys shadowing me. At home. That's off the reservation, out of bounds."

He tried to stifle a grin. "Who was it you think you saw?"

"The one with the pole up his ass."

"Weaver, you mean?" he said.

"I've seen my share of strange cops, that guy's one of them."

"Really? Thanks so much for the personnel eval."

"Just so we're clear, it *was* Weaver," I said.

"Then I'll have to dress him down, won't I? Meantime, you get the hell out of here, this is a crime scene. Unless you'd like another ride into town."

"Okay, yeah, okay. Just keep your men off my ass."

Then I took his suggestion. I got on my bike and got the hell out of there.

19

A Georgia State Trooper followed me as I pulled away from the bridge. I was headed into New Bethany and figured he was on some other business – maybe a court date, maybe lunch. But the way he was following wasn't right – when I slowed, he slowed; I sped up, he sped up. He hung back, maintaining a steady distance.

We played the game for several miles before he turned on his lights and siren, gunned it, and went roaring past. He gave me the cold stare as he went by.

State Troopers were good at that – the cold stare – so I didn't make much of this one. It was part of their DNA. Not long ago I'd watched a half-dozen of them swapping Polaroids of bloody highway wrecks like trading cards: "Here, you take this headless woman, give me that guy sliced in half on the train track."

To get into that club you had to have a strong stomach.

I hadn't realized where I was, but I was approaching the road that ran down to the Rollings house. Back on Sunday, I'd taken the Interstate down and had come in from the west. This was the back way in; the way, most likely, the shooter had come. I still had time before meeting Scotts and decided on a quick swing by the crime scene.

I turned down the road and slowed. The sun was moving toward the top of the sky, above the tall pines. As I approached the Rollings place, I saw a dusty yellow sedan hurriedly backing out of the drive.

It whipped out, kicked back gravel as it jerked forward, and sped past me.

It was a yellow Cadillac. An older model. The car Will Black had just described. The driver was doing his best to conceal his face, but he was a big man – big and burly.

I considered going back to the bridge to tell Black about the Caddy but decided against it. I was now more interested in where the car had come from and what it had been doing there. I continued to the Rollings house.

I nosed the bike into the drive. The house was dark, nothing stirring inside. I eased further down the drive and saw a small blond boy out on the back lawn, far behind the house. It was the child I'd seen through the window Sunday morning. He seemed to be wandering aimlessly, slowly, in the general vicinity of where Rollings' body had been. His father's body.

I revved the bike to sound my presence, then shut it down and slid off. The boy turned toward me. I waved down to him. He stared back, showing nothing. Bright blond hair, a blank face. He didn't seem frightened, just vacant.

I was about to shout something down to him when the door at the front of the house opened. The woman I'd assumed to be Mrs. Rollings stood there. She wore a long, royal blue satin robe sashed tightly around her slender waist. Her hair was disheveled, but her face was perfectly made.

"Yes?" the woman said coldly.

"Are you Mrs. Rollings?"

She said nothing, stared at me.

"I'm Gil Coates with *The Atlanta Democrat*, ma'am. I am very sorry to bother you, I realize this is an awful time." I moved closer to her, extended my press card. "I stopped in to offer our condolences and to ask if we could arrange for an interview sometime in the future. Not today or tomorrow, much later. Our paper would like to do a tribute article on Mr. Rollings, if you didn't mind. He was an important man in Atlanta."

She looked at me with tortured eyes. "Come in," she said and disappeared inside, leaving the door open.

I glanced back at the boy. He was still standing, frozen, staring toward me.

Inside the house was dim, lit only by the sunlight filtering in through the heavily draped windows. I stood in the foyer but didn't see Mrs. Rollings. I called to her.

"In here, please," she said in that low, husky voice I'd overheard the other day. I stepped through a door and saw her sitting in a formal living room on a large Victorian sofa. She sat upright and stiff. She had lit a cigarette.

"Sit down, if you please," she said, exhaling cigarette smoke.

"Thank you." I put my card on the table beside her and took a chair.

She studied me as she continued smoking. After a moment, she flicked her ash toward an ash tray on the table beside her and asked softly, "What is it you want to know about Bobby?"

"Yes ma'am…ah, may I take notes?"

"Of course. How else would you remember what I say?"

"Yes ma'am –"

"Though I guess what you'd really like to know is who killed him. Is that true?"

"Yes ma'am, that's true, but isn't that a question for the police?"

"They will do nothing. They're afraid." She watched my reaction carefully, then turned away, took another deep draw on her cigarette and again flicked ashes.

She turned back to me. A vague smile hung around her face. I remembered looking through the curtains the day of the murder and seeing this woman, so beautiful, even in her suffering of the moment. I looked at her now, up close, and saw I'd underestimated that beauty. She was unnervingly gorgeous. The kind you don't just see, you feel, too. And smell. And want to touch. The deadly kind.

She gazed at me intensely, as if trying to read my mind. "You see me like all the rest, a beautiful and crazy woman. Am I right?"

"I imagine you're very distraught, yes ma'am, after what you've been through. I'm so sorry for your loss."

I returned her smile then looked quickly down to my note pad. "I wonder if I could ask…is that your son outside, out in back?"

"Is that where he is? Oh. But, yes, that's him, Robert Rollings. The third."

I made the note.

"I just asked," she continued, "if you want to know who killed my husband."

"If you want to tell me."

She looked away, gazing down the room at a large portrait of an older couple that hung on the far wall over the mantel. She pointed to the picture.

"Him," she said. She began a barely audible laugh and that wispy smile returned to her face as she stared, entranced, at the portrait.

I sat silent, allowing her to continue. She said nothing, sat gazing at the picture.

"Who is that?" I asked.

She turned and stared wide-eyed.

"I don't know," she said. She turned back to the portrait, without blinking.

"You don't know who that is?"

She stood abruptly. "I thought I did, but I did not."

She walked into the foyer, flung her cigarette out the front door, returned to the room and stood at the sofa. Her satin robe had fallen partly open to reveal a soft, alabaster skin and the hint of her bosom.

She sat and tried to regain her composure.

"Of course I know who that is. He's my grandfather. And that woman is my grandmother. She is very kind and quite crazy. Only, she is dotty crazy. Not like him. He is evil."

"You suspect he had something to do with your husband's death?"

"No, Mr…" she reached over and picked up the card I'd sat on the table. "No, Mr. Coates, Assignments Reporter for *The Atlanta Democrat,* I don't suspect anything. I *know* it."

I fumbled with my notebook, jotted something, "Why would he do that?"

"Well," she said coyly, "I can tell you but you can't write it down, it has to be, you know . . . ah . . ."

"Off the record?"

"Yes, off the record. I don't want to get him in trouble."

"I see. You don't want to get your grandfather in trouble."

"Don't you understand? He killed Bobby – Bobby the booby, the dumb bastard. He didn't need to. It would have been so simple. Let him see the damn boy. Let him *have* him for that matter, if he wanted him that bad. Let him *have* him!"

She was near hysteria now.

"My grandfather could do things for us – things Bobby could never do." She took a deep breath, then several more, drawing her composure. "Do you have any idea who that man is?" She pointed to the picture. "Any idea?"

My thoughts turned to the boy outside, alone out here with this obviously unstable woman. "Mrs. Rollings, are you and your son alone right now?"

"What do you mean by that?" she snapped. "What are you intending to do?"

She edged back on the sofa, wrapped her arms around herself.

"No, oh no, ma'am. I'm not going to do anything. I'm was concerned that you need your parents here…or someone…"

"To comfort me? You think I need comfort?"

"It might help. This is a horrible thing that's happened. I'm surprised you are alone out here."

"I do not need comfort. That is the last thing I need."

"But—"

"What I need is for you to leave immediately. Please leave. . ." Her voice trailed off. She buried her face in her hands. She began to weep.

"Yes, ma'am. I'll leave now. I'm so sorry to have intruded. It was not right. I apologize. I promise you, nothing you have said to me will be printed. Absolutely nothing."

"What?" She looked up furiously. "You won't put it in the paper? You won't tell them my grandfather killed my husband? I told you he did. I told the police he did. I told everyone he did. Nobody will listen to me. He killed my husband and nobody will listen. Get out of here, right now. Get out!"

She jumped up and came at me. She loosened her robe and let it fall open, revealing her naked body. She seethed, "Now you get out of here this second, before I get you in real trouble. And if you don't think I will, try me."

I stood up and pulled out the small tape recorder. I held it up so she could see the green light blinking. That stopped her tirade. She glared at me with the ferocity of a madwoman.

"As I promised, Mrs. Rollings, nothing you have said to me today will be printed."

She glared, her eyes braced for violence. She raised her arm slowly, pointed a finger at me and whispered, "DeRussey."

"What?"

"You'll find out."

"What do you mean, Mrs. Rollings?"

"DeRussey, that's where you're headed." She glowered then lowered her arm. She relaxed her stare and her face went suddenly serene.

I held her eyes a moment more then hurried out of the house to my bike. As I cranked it, I watched her stand in the door, alone, robe hanging open now, revealing an elegantly turned body and, on her face, the most innocent smile in the world.

Out on the back lawn, the boy stood in the same place, facing up the drive toward me, his blue angelic eyes fixed on nothing.

As I sped toward New Bethany, I made a mental note to ask Scotts what "DeRussey" meant. Was it a local reference?

But even before that, I was going to tell Chief Black about the yellow Caddy I'd seen. Twice in the last thirty minutes. First, as it sped away from the Rollings house as I approached. And then again, just now – as I passed it, tucked away in a small thicket of trees just off the highway, the perfect vantage to monitor traffic to and from the Rollings place.

20

Scotts was leaning against her Jeep with arms crossed and a troubled look on her face as I rolled into the Sheriff's parking lot. I pulled into the spot next to her and tugged my helmet off. When she recognized me she straightened and stepped over to the bike. Her troubled face began glowing.

"Hey, nifty! What is that…What does that say, Bonneville?" She eyed the bike admiringly front to back. "Take me for a spin?"

"Not today," I said, dismounting. "What's with the sour puss when I pulled in?"

"What? Oh, that, yeah…sorry. Hey look, I can't work for you anymore. On this story, I mean. It's my husband…AND my dad. Both of them. They say I have to quit."

"You're kidding."

She shook her head, flung her palms open, exasperated. "Will Black said *something* to my dad that spooked him, and then Dad said something to Travis, and now Travis says I have to quit. They say it's…it's 'too dangerous' is all he says. Just this morning Travis told me. Like, an hour ago."

She had a conflicted look – half angry, half heartbroken. She was a smart woman, long on ambition, and this wasn't sitting well.

"Look, any story can be dangerous. If you aren't a little scared, you're probably not onto anything."

"I know, I know. But Travis is adamant. He's scared for me, he is. I have to go along or he will be pissed – I mean, *really, really.*"

"Okay. If that's the deal, that's the deal." I looked away for a minute then back. "I'm sorry."

"I'll keep working on him," she said. "Maybe he'll give me a little rope. I don't know. I'll call you if anything changes."

"Sure. I hope you can find a way." I extended my hand and she shook it with a clasp of determination.

"I hope… he's hard headed, though."

"I understand." I turned toward the bike.

"Will Black is who had them call me," she said.

"What do you mean?"

"You asked me to find out who told Boyd O'Con to call me to pick you up. It was Will Black. He told Boyd to call me, said I'd be a good one to call, I could take you back to your car. He also said that I could tell you more than he could."

"That's what he said?"

"That's what he said, according to Boyd. Pretty weird, huh? Will Black's the one who put us together, now he's breaking up the band."

"Yeah. . . strange. Thanks."

"Oh, and Bobby Rolling's funeral is Saturday. First Baptist Church, downtown, right over there on the corner. Everyone will be there," she said. She pointed toward the church and gave me a knowing nod.

"Everyone?"

"Everyone. Including the man who killed him, Jacob Lacobee."

"I keep telling you, you don't know that."

"No, *you* don't know it. Everybody else does," she said. "Look, I gotta go."

"One more thing. You ever heard of something called 'DeRussey'?"

She screwed her ruby lips around and furrowed her brow. She looked off a moment then shook her head.

"I don't think so. What is it?"

"No idea."

"Another mystery?"

"Looks like it.

"I'll ask around for you. No harm in that, huh?"

She stepped back to her Jeep and pointed to my bike as she climbed in. "You owe me a ride, if you remember!"

21

WHILE I was there, I stuck my head in the Sheriff's Department. I wanted to see if Will Black had made it back from the bridge and if they'd found anything in the river. I also wanted to mention the yellow Cadillac I'd seen at the Rollings house and, shortly afterward, hidden in the trees.

The guy at the dispatch desk – his name plate said "O'Con" so I assumed this was Scotts' cousin, Boyd – said Will Black was out. He had no idea when he'd return. He limited the remainder of his responses to grunts, nods and head shakes.

As I was leaving the building, a patrol car pulled into the parking lot. It was Deputy Weaver. I walked over and met him as he stepped out of his vehicle.

"Deputy Weaver, remember me? Coates, with *The Democrat*?" I handed him my card.

He pulled his dark glasses off and squinted through slits for eyes. "You were at the shooting Sunday morning."

"That was me. I didn't get a chance to thank you."

He looked puzzled. "How's that?"

"You got me hauled in by Will Black. What a pleasure that was." He stifled a smile.

"I've seen you somewhere else, haven't I?" I asked.

"How would I know that?" Weaver said.

"You go up to Atlanta now and then?"

"No, I don't," he said sharply. "Now excuse me, I've got reports to fill in."

He started away then paused. "You know, Chief went a lot easier on you than he should have."

He resumed toward the building and took a glance back as he opened the door. I saluted him cordially.

Despite the denial, I was almost certain he'd been the one following me – either him or one of Will Black's other minions. And I found it hard to believe a small town deputy, by mere coincidence, had official business in Atlanta that time of night.

There'd been the other tails, the other cops, too. And since I wasn't buying Will Black's "protection" claims, that left the question: What the hell were they doing?

22

I reported to Mr. Manship's residence at nine that evening as arranged. The always-punctilious Mrs. Christian ushered me into his study.

"What's our story, Mr. Coates?" he asked, pointing me to the leather chair opposite him. He offered me a cigar and a drink. I declined both.

I updated him on every new detail of the Rollings killing, including Gary Hooper's information that Rollings and the bank that employed him were under investigation by the DOJ. And that he, Mr. Manship, sat on the board of that bank.

"Yes, I do," he said, smiling, drawing a puff on his cigar.

He asked nothing more about the Rollings story. He turned the conversation to the upcoming Democratic National Convention, set for this summer in Atlanta. He was concerned about the chaos, maybe even violence that might grow out of the conflict between camps of the two party frontrunners – Michael Dukakis, an East Coast liberal and Jesse Jackson, a black Southern populist.

"There are worse things, but I'm afraid there can be *too much* democracy," he said. "Of course there can be too much of *anything* – except time, money, clarity and beautiful women."

I promptly agreed.

"Our founders didn't just *forget* to give women, blacks and the indentured the right to vote, you know. Many wanted to limit participation to property holders and well-educated. That republic would be quite different from the one we now inhabit, don't you think?"

"Yes, sir, I'm sure it would."

"Yes, well, in any case," he sighed and slapped his hands to his knees, "you're not on the editorial board, so you don't have to listen to my ramblings about all that."

He rose from his chair. I stood and waited further instruction.

He looked me square in the eye. "I am on the Georgia Commerce Bank board. I'm on any number of boards, profit and non-profit. I'm on the hospital board. I'm on the University Board of Regents. Lots of boards. It's what's expected of me."

"Yes, sir. I have wondered why you would be so interested in this story. Now I see the connection."

"No, Mr. Coates, not yet you don't. But it'll become clear soon enough."

He shook my hand pleasantly and called for Mrs. Christian to show me out. It was a long, silent walk to the door.

23

By the time I got back to my apartment that night I was physically and mentally spent.

All that quickly changed when I opened the door to find a naked woman in my bed. Well, almost naked, but for a sheer nighty that was at least two sizes too small.

"Hi, Coates. Come get me," Lacey whispered in her whoriest voice.

"I love your nighttime voice," I managed to mutter as my clothes began to fly off.

"I love your mark," she said and kissed the scar above my left eyebrow. "Tell me how you got it.'

"I've told you a dozen times."

"Oh that's right, you have."

We wasted no more time on small talk.

An hour later we came up for air.

"So you *don't* have another girlfriend," she said, smiling, lighting a cigarette.

"You could tell?"

"A wild guess. You on a big story? That what's keeping you away from me?"

"Maybe."

"Tell me about it?"

"Can't right now."

"I see," she smiled again and drew a puff. "You only want to *ask* the questions?"

I took her cigarette and drew a puff. I hadn't intended to ask anything, but since she brought it up.

"Is your office investigating any Atlanta banks or bankers for anything?"

"Fuck, Coates, the DA is always investigating banks and bankers – for just about everything. What kind of dumbass question is that?"

"Would you know if the Feds were?"

She eyed me suspiciously, pursed her lips.

"This is not a trick question," I said. But it was. I already knew from Gary Hooper that the DOJ *did* have an investigation of Rollings' bank underway. I wanted to know how quiet they were keeping it. That would suggest how deep it ran.

"I don't know. That's a bunch of high and mighty pricks over there at Justice. They don't come around our place much. Sure as hell don't talk to junior staff. But my bosses would know," Lacey said. "We have a liaison who keeps them connected to the Feds."

"What if I had a specific name?"

"Then maybe I could kiss a specific ass and find out more," she said.

"You sure that's all you'd do?"

"For you, I'd do anything." She gave me a mocking grin, leaving no doubt she was largely lying.

"Bobby Rollings, Jr.," I said. "That's the name."

She fell silent and stared at me. There was a hint of alarm in her eyes. They showed that little nervous tremor every time she got aroused, or, like now, got concerned.

"What?" I said. "You know something, don't you? You know the name?"

She sat for a moment and collected herself. "I've heard the name in the office. Saw it on the case list. That's the dead guy, right? Killed a few days ago?"

"Easter Sunday."

"Sure. That one. We're investigating the murder. It's not our jurisdiction, but he was from Atlanta, right? An assets manager, investment banker of some kind? That why you asked about the bank investigation?"

"Right." I sensed she was holding back. "You know, Lace, you seem to know a lot about this. More than you're telling. What gives?"

"It's not my case," she said, shaking her head and rolling out of bed. She started dressing. "Not even my department."

"So don't ask."

"That's right, don't ask."

"Okay. So you're leaving now, right?"

"You know, Coates, you're some sharp investigator."

"So I've been told. Can I ask one more thing?"

"Can I stop you?"

"No."

She stared off, silently.

"Would you tell me if I was about to step into hot water?"

A softness broke across her face. She leaned in to me and kissed my cheek. Then my scar. It felt like a moment of actual endearment.

"You never get out of it, sweetheart. My boss still wants to cook your ass for those notes he subpoenaed on the Martin deal."

"I didn't have any notes. I told him that."

"So you said. In any case, when you're about to step in the deep *shit,* I *will* tell you."

She pulled me to her and kissed me for about a half hour more.

"How was that for a long goodbye?" she said in a throaty half-whisper.

"Have I told you I love your nighttime voice, Lace? I wish you'd leave it here tonight."

"I know you do. But I have to go."

"So, by not warning me now, you're saying—"

"I'm saying goodnight."

She threw a bye-bye wave over her shoulder and was out the door.

24

I spent the next two days typing up my notes, reading clips in our morgue, checking in with key sources and making discreet inquiries around town. I was trying to get a picture of the dead guy, Rollings.

He was, as Scotts had said, a Junior, which made his kid Robert Rollings, III. His parents were both dead, and he'd been an only child so he had no immediate relatives.

He had begun his career in Atlanta as a junior corporate lawyer, right out of Virginia Law School. Three years later, and immediately after his marriage to Lorelei Lacobee, he had moved into the investment brokering business.

Their marriage had been a big to-do in Atlanta social circles. Hosted at Montrose Plantation, with many Atlanta A-listers on hand, it got a two-page spread in our society section. The big event, according to our society editor who "simply could not have missed it for the world," set her family back a million bucks. "Or more," the grand dame of our social pages added with a wink.

Rollings moved up the investment world ladder fast, owing in part to the book of Lacobee business he'd taken to one of the high-stakes Atlanta investment firms. After a couple of years there, he moved to Georgia Commerce Bank, where Lacobee sat on the board. He'd been there until his murder.

The scuttlebutt was he was a sharp cookie, charismatic, and a skirt chaser. And sometimes a pants chaser. But, he didn't drink or drug, according to those who knew those kinds of things.

Bobby Rollings had also been a rising star in Greater Atlanta social circles, though his wife had never quite fit in. Few had kind words for her – other than about her amazing beauty: She was considered unpolished, reckless and boorish. But for her grandfather's money, she would never have been admitted to The Club. Her sexual appetites were said to be more insatiable than her husband's. And some said that while Bobby was a charming though nefarious character, Lorelei was a schizophrenic and psychopath. She was more than capable of killing her husband, they believed.

Apparently, Robert and Lorelei Rollings had not had the most enviable union in town.

I also devoted a generous amount of time to making Lacey happy. I got a special reward for my efforts. After the second night of romping around in my bed, she answered my question.

"Here's the deal," she said, firing up a cigarette. "We – we being you're local District Attorney's Office – *are i*nvestigating the Bobby Rollings killing. Actually, we're helping out, at the request of the Latham County DA. Even though he was killed down there, since he resided in Atlanta, we're in on it."

"You told me that two days ago."

She leaned in and kissed my ear then whispered, "Shhhh, there's more."

I shhhhed.

"The Georgia Attorney General is *also* investigating the case. But their investigation focuses on the bank Rollings worked for, not the murder. That investigation was already in progress when he was killed. Do you know which bank that is? Your paper's bank. The one your boss sits on the board of."

"And you already knew all that," I said. "You knew it the other night when I asked."

"Yes." She turned away, focusing on her cigarette and the wisps of smoke rising from the tip. "We're working with the State Attorney General."

She threw me a sideways glance. "And *maybe* I am working on that case a little. On the fringe. Out on the very edge. But, it's not what you think. When you asked—"

"I see."

"I didn't lie to you, Coates. I recall very damn clearly what I said, and it wasn't— "

"That's good because we do have this deal."

"I know the deal," she said.

"*Little lies okay, big deceits not okay*. It's *your* deal."

"I may have *slightly* lied. I came nowhere near deceit."

"Fine. I take your word for it, Lace. I do. So, what about the Feds?"

"Okay, on that. . . if my bosses know anything about a DOJ investigation of Rollings, or Georgia Commerce Bank, they're denying it. And honestly, if there is one, I don't think they know about it. I've played with them long enough to know when they're gaming me, and neither of them knows anything about a federal investigation."

"And the State Attorney General, would they know?"

"No. They don't know anything about a federal investigation either."

"And you are certain?"

"I am."

"I won't ask how."

"You shouldn't."

There was my answer. The Department of Justice investigation Hooper was covering ran silent and ran deep here in Georgia. That meant they were drop-dead serious about it. This was apparently something big – too big to let the state in on.

Some big name, or some several big names, were the targets.

Maybe Emily Scott was smart to quit. Maybe this *was* a risky story, as her husband feared. But if the DOJ investigation was behind Will Black's warnings, it begged the question: How would a small-town cop have wind of a federal investigation that the Georgia A.G. knew nothing about?

That didn't jibe.

25

T HE First Baptist Church of New Bethany was filled to overflow-
ing. It looked like nothing but locals – the beholden and the
curious. The Rev. Thomas Greene stood at the pulpit in a circle of
light, his face somber, lips pursed, a bible clutched in both hands.
He asked for a moment of silent prayer and bowed his head.

After the silence, a small choir sang a few stanzas of the hymn
This is the Day the Lord Hath Made. It seemed an odd choice for a
funeral service.

The music ended and Rev. Greene looked up and gazed across
the congregation. He straightened himself, eyes strong, as if he
would soon lift the world onto his shoulders and did not intend
to drop it.

In an orotund voice he spoke: "Weep, brethren, weep. Weep
if you will. Dry your hearts out. Adversity strikes us all in our
lifetime. God knows we have feet of clay. Jesus Christ knows our
grief and our terror. Jesus wept. We may weep."

He waved his hand across the congregation and the single circle
of light that had been on him widened and brightened, lighting the
full congregation.

Four figures on the front row stood out in blazing silhouette.
In the middle was Jacob Lacobee, a tall, silver-haired man who,
though seventy-one years old, stood sturdy and erect, immovable
and immutable. Clinging to him on his right was his wife, Eva

Lacobee, her head bowed. She held a delicate handkerchief with which she gently patted her breast. The small blond boy, Robert Rollings, III, stood to Lacobee's left, clinging to his side. To the child's left was Lorelei Rollings, attired in tragic black. She stood a pace apart from the boy and her grandparents.

The minister waved his hand to sit then resumed. He aimed his words right at the widow.

"Robert Rollings was a good man. A good husband. A good father. Yes, son," he turned his eyes to the boy, "your father was a good man."

The minister went on and on for some time, singing the praises of Bobby Rollings, mixing in verses from Psalms and concluding by leading the small choir in a reprise of *This is the Day the Lord Hath Made.*

My attention shifted from the minister to the congregation – first to a study of Lorelei Rollings and then to her grandfather. The distance between them, though only a few feet, was palpable; she sat stiff and tense, angled away, head turned from him and the boy. She never turned in their direction. Lacobee himself moved only once during the service – a small almost imperceptible turn of his head toward the boy and a gentle reach behind the child's back to pull him closer.

Scotts was in the congregation. She sat with her husband, Travis, only a few pews from the bereaved family. Her choice of seating gave her clear sight of the family – a choice I suspected she had not made by accident.

The service concluded and the casket was ushered solemnly down the aisle. Jacob Lacobee marched immediately behind it, his wife, the boy and now even Lorelei Rollings clinging to him.

I had been sitting at the rear of the church and was able to get out to the foyer ahead of the rush. I found an out-of-the-way spot and watched the wave of congregants push by. I hoped to catch Scotts and ask if she'd heard anything new.

She saw me, waved her husband on his way, gave him a sweet parting kiss, and hurried over.

"They found the gun," she whispered, almost breathless with enthusiasm. "They can match it. A 12-guage shotgun." She pulled me further away from the exodus. "They've got a trace on it, and I think they already know who owns it. That's what I think. I'll know more by morning."

"Wait a sec, I thought you quit."

"That's another thing. I'm not. Well, sort of not. As far as some people go, I am. As far as other people go – that's you – I'm not."

"Where does Travis stand?"

"He's okay, he's with me now. It took some doing, but you know men, stick a couple of knockers in their face at the right time, they'll agree to anything."

Who could resist a laugh at that? I couldn't.

"What about your father?"

"Couldn't work the knockers on Dad, for god's sake! Ew! As far as he knows, I'm quit."

"That could get tricky."

"Nah," she waved the idea off, glanced over at the crowd pushing their way out of the church. "I can handle it."

"If you think so."

"I do think so. So now, there's more." She pulled me further aside.

"You asked me about 'DeRussey'? Found this out. This is creepy. DeRussey is where they're burying Rollings this afternoon. It's the family cemetery on the plantation. Located way far back somewhere, hidden. Here's the creepy part: It's over a hundred years old and supposedly includes some people – some of them plantation hands, they say – who have disappeared over the years. They say when the Lacobees need to solve a problem, that's how they do it. They – poof! – vanish it! That's the 'Lacobee Solution' – that's what my dad and grandparents and all them call it. The 'Lacobee Solution.' You know, sometimes I wish I had a solution like that. Don't you? Anyhow, that's the story, even though I can't find anyone who's ever seen the place. Not even my cop friends. So who knows? Except, that is where they're burying Rollings today."

Out of the shadows, Will Black appeared. His jowly face was red with annoyance.

"Morning, Chief Black," Scotts said. "He was just asking how to get to the graveside service."

"I can help you with that," he said and turned to me. "You go west six miles, then up onto the interstate straight back to Atlanta."

"I was planning to attend the graveside—"

"No, you weren't. Private service, you're not invited. So get on your way." He turned back to Scotts. "And you. Does your daddy know you're talking to this guy? I was told you didn't work with him any more."

"Ah…yes and no. I mean, I still work for the paper. I still have my job. What I do now is provide background info, that's all. Help identify who's who. Give directions when needed."

"Is that so?"

"Yep. As so as so can be. No field work, nothing dangerous, just background stuff. Stuff like that."

Will Black stared at her and shook his head. "Sister, if you don't think I know a load of baloney when I see it. . ."

"I know you do, Chief, but Daddy—"

"I've told him this is not a good idea. And I'm telling you. After this, I'm done with advice. I won't say another word to your daddy or you. If you get yourself killed in all this mess, don't come crying to me."

Will Black stood there, determined to stare her down. I figured she'd be able to hold her own in a face-off, so rather than be stuck for hours, I intervened.

"Are you still looking for that yellow car?"

"Maybe," he said. He swung his eyes to me, surprised, like he'd forgotten he'd told me.

"I saw one right after I saw you and your boys dragging the river the other day. Big yellow Cadillac, I'm almost sure. Older model. I saw it twice. First down by the Rollings house, pulling out of the drive. Broad daylight. It shot right past me in a big hurry. Half an hour later it was hiding back in the trees off Highway 37. Looked to me like the driver was watching traffic to the Rollings place."

"That's what you saw, huh?"

"I thought you should know about it."

"That's being a damn good citizen, by golly. I'll have to remember that." He pointed his finger at Scotts. "And you remember what I just said – don't come crying to me."

He walked away.

Scotts looked at me. "Did he really say that? 'If you get killed, don't come crying to me?'" She screwed her face into a contortion of bug-eyed silliness.

"He was serious. You sure you want to re-up?"

"I'm not scared. I don't know why, I've just never been a scaredy person." She beamed ear to ear. "I like that about me. Good for you?"

"Yep. Let's go get coffee."

26

SIDEBAR:
"Georgia Farmers in High Cotton"

Excerpt: *The Atlanta Democrat, September 6, 1987*

ATLANTA, Ga. – Despite early concerns of a global commodity glut, Georgia cotton farmers are posting a banner year for crop production and prices, according to the Georgia Crop Reporting Service. This marks a third straight year of gains, after nearly three decades of losing acreage and production.

"Cotton producers are not out of the woods yet," said state Agriculture Commissioner Jay Bowen, "but these are good signs. Farmers are making money again. Acreage in production is growing and per bale prices are well up over last year."

While total production numbers for the year aren't final, Bowen estimates Georgia farmers have produced some 1.9 million bales on some 2.3 million acres.

"Those are the preliminary numbers, and if they hold, which we think they will, this will be the third straight year of five percent growth," he said.

Bowen attributes the turnaround in cotton production to the move to corporate farming. Much of the cotton in the state today is being produced by agribusinesses that manage large tracts of land. That, along with advances in mechanization, a recent breakthrough in boll weevil control and federally funded farm aid programs have made cotton farming the realm of big business.

Not everyone is completely happy about that. Independent cotton growers see it as good-news-bad-news.

"Cotton farming ain't for small farmers anymore," said Jacob Lacobee, one of the state's largest independent growers. He has been farming cotton for over fifty years and currently is chairman of the Georgia Independent Growers Association.

"The big corporations are taking over," he said. "And even though it's true the cotton business is getting to be better, and we are finally making a living wage at it, it's coming at a price for us independents."

What price is that?

"The end of our farms, that's what," Lacobee says.

27

"No time like the present," Scotts said at the coffee shop, agreeing that we should interview Jacob Lacobee that afternoon, right after the graveside service, right there at his home. "He told me the other day 'come anytime.' Now is anytime, right?"

A media ambush isn't always sporting, but sometimes to get the truth you have to trick it out. It's not an uncommon technique. Ask any cop. Or lawyer.

"Let's go," I said.

We took her Jeep out to Montrose and parked off the road beside a small grove of pines, about a quarter mile from the main gate. We watched as the few invitees to the graveside service trickled out of the grounds one by one. Chief Black and Deputy Weaver were the last to leave. After they pulled away, the grounds fell still and silent.

The only ones left at the main house, by Scotts' guess, would be Jacob Lacobee, his wife, Lorelei Rollings and her son, and a kitchen maid or two.

"Let's leave the car here and walk," she said. "It's a half mile in from the gate."

The place had an air of antiquity. Ancient oaks canopied the winding entrance drive. A cool southerly stirred the trees and the decades of dust accumulated on a working plantation.

The lush front lawn stretched out in all directions. It was perfectly mown. Neatly trimmed ground covers, in a variety of variegated greens, flowed among the trees, edging bed after bed of azaleas in pinks and whites and lavenders. Alcoves with white trellises, benches and fountains were tucked quietly away among copse of crepe myrtles and manicured hedges. The entire front grounds looked like somebody's idea of the Garden of Eden. Somebody with lots of staff.

The "Big House," as Scotts called it, was equally impressive. It was a sprawling white two-storied wooden structure with a half-dozen chimneys lifting into the sky and a deep porch that circled the house. It seemed the size of a major municipal building. Scotts said it was at least a hundred years old, maybe more.

She pushed the door bell and a genteel chime echoed within.

In time, Eva Lacobee came to the door, still in her dark funeral dress. She hurriedly unwrapped an apron as she looked at us. After a moment of indecision, she held it behind her back, mannerly.

"Why. . . we weren't expecting anyone. . . I. . .can I help you?"

"Yes ma'am, Miss Eva," Scotts said. "I'm Emily Scott from in town. I spoke with Mister Jacob two days ago about an interview. About this awful tragedy you and your family have had. He said anytime was convenient to visit him, and we just wondered—"

"I didn't hear anyone drive in."

"No ma'am, we walked in from the road. This is such a beautiful place, we wanted to take it in."

"Yes, well, thank you—"

"And we came to offer our condolences. Oh, my manners – this is Gil Coates, from Atlanta. He's with the newspaper up there. We both are."

"Oh, I see. . . but I'm afraid this is not a good time. We just returned from a funeral. This is not a good time at all."

"Yes ma'am, of course not. It's just that Mister Jacob told me to come out anytime."

"Well, he isn't here right now. He just rode out to check on the nigras. He won't be back until supper."

I piped up. "Your azaleas are so beautiful, Mrs. Lacobee, considering the cool spring we're having."

She eyed me with uncertainty. "Yes, thank you. They're especially nice this year. I keep them covered when it's chilled. They bloomed two days before Easter."

"Right on schedule."

"Yes. But about your visit with Jacob, this is not—"

"You're right, ma'am," I said. "We know this is not the best time. It's just that we have our deadlines and we got the idea that Mr. Lacobee had something important he wanted to tell us. We're with the newspaper, and we're trying to write about what a sad tragedy this has been for your family. Such an important family in Georgia. He seemed like he wanted to say something about it."

There was a sharp, banging noise from inside the house and Mrs. Lacobee turned abruptly. "One moment, please excuse me," she said to us.

She hurried away, leaving the entrance door ajar. We looked into the hall that ran through the center of the house. At the far end stood the boy, looking toward the front door, straight at us. Like I'd seen earlier, he seemed to be staring blankly, seeing nothing.

Mrs. Lacobee padded back to the door, calling over her shoulder, "Put plenty of butter in the bottom of that pan, Lucy."

She had gathered a composure she hadn't been able to find earlier. She looked at Scotts. "You're the Adams girl, aren't you?"

"Yes ma'am, I was before I got married. Buddy Adams' daughter. I went to school with Lorelei – high school, that is," Scotts said.

"I thought you were familiar."

"Yes ma'am. I came out here once or twice when she had a party. That was a while ago."

"I see." She studied Scotts carefully. "I saw you at the service today, didn't I? Thank you for coming. But. . .I don't know when Jacob will be back. I suppose you can wait here on the porch if you'd like. There's a nice sitting over there. With a swing. I'll tell him you're here when he returns."

"Yes ma'am," Scotts said. "We'll do that. We'll sit over there, wait for him and enjoy your beautiful place."

"That'll be fine," she said and started to close the door. She hesitated a moment, then spoke. "I'll just say that I hope they catch the nigra that did this. And I hope they do I-don't-know-what to him!"

"Yes ma'am," Scotts said. "Do they know a nigra did it?"

"I don't know if *they* do, but *I* do. What else would do something like that to a person on Easter Sunday? And with that baby standing right there beside him! THAT BABY WAS STANDING RIGHT THERE BESIDE HIS DADDY! He hasn't spoken a word since then. He looks at you, then it's like he doesn't see you, like you were vanishing before his little eyes. God deliver his little soul!"

"That's terrible, Miss Eva," Scotts said. "He must be in shock."

"He's seen the very devil himself, that's what. The very devil himself!" She started to weep. "I hope they cut his head off, that's what. If there's a God in Heaven, that's what he'll do. You know he will!"

"Now Miss Eva, you shouldn't work yourself into something," Scotts said and reached a calming hand toward the trembling woman's arm.

The old woman drew the arm to her chest then crossed both tightly. "He won't let it pass unanswered. He won't, I promise you. He won't tolerate it. Not to us. He will not let this pass unanswered."

Scotts and I stood there in silence. There was a door slam from deep within the house. Eva Lacobee began to compose herself. She clutched at the door, pulling herself into balance. She looked at us, eyes flowing in emotion. "Not to us."

"Eva!" came a call from inside the house. It was a man's voice, deep and resonant.

"That's Jacob," she said dabbing her face in her sleeve. As she eased the door closed she said, "I. . .I'll tell him you're here."

28

WE took seats on the porch and waited. Scotts fiddled with her large bag, retrieved a notepad and pen from somewhere down in its depths. She laid them across her lap.

In a half hour or so, Jacob Lacobee came around the corner of the house, a rifle laid over his shoulder. He had the young boy with him and was holding him close with a tight hand.

Lacobee took a careful look at us as he and the boy came up the steps, onto the porch and over to us. We stood to meet him.

Scotts was the first to extend her hand. "Hello, Mr. Lacobee, I'm Emily—"

"I know who you are. The both of you. Remember you from the other day. You're Buddy Adams' girl. And you, you must be Adam Manship's hand. That about right?"

I nodded and extended my hand. "I work for his paper, yes sir. Gil Coates, with the *Atlanta Democrat.*"

"Like I said, Adam's hand." He kept the rifle on his shoulder, his right hand up near the trigger guard. He didn't seem in the mood to let go of the boy or the gun for a handshake.

"Yes, sir. We wanted to ask you a few—"

"Before you go any further, remind me, what do I say to bind you not to print my words?"

"You would tell us, 'This is off the record', Mister Jacob," Scotts answered immediately.

"Okay, then. Consider it told."

"Completely off the record, then," I said and nodded.

Scotts stuffed the notepad and pen back in her bag, looked up at him and smiled coquettishly.

"Off the record, Mister Jacob," she added.

"Good. Just a second, now." He leaned down to the boy and pointed toward the porch swing across the way. "You go on over there and swing, Bobby, while I talk to these people."

The boy did as instructed.

"So you know Mr. Manship?" I asked.

"That's right."

"How's that, if you don't mind my asking?"

"I do mind." He swung his stare to Scotts. "You have some questions?"

The sway of his gaze caught her off guard for a moment. But not for long. "So, what happened to Bobby Rollings, do you think, Mister Jacob?"

He smiled at her and winked. "Looks like he got shot, for one thing. Too bad."

"Too bad?" she said.

"That's what I said. Hellfire, anybody coulda seen that comin'. That boy wadn't too bright."

"He seemed successful," I said. "Lawyer, investment banker. But he wasn't too smart you say?"

"No, he wadn't."

"How was that?" I asked.

"Well," he flashed a codger-coy grin, "I 'spect you and Adam already know the answer to that. Adam sure does. Ask him, you don't believe me. That boy stole money everywhere he went. Stole from some nuns and got them federal boys on his tail. Stole from that bunch of rich niggers up there in Atlanta. Even stole from me. I'd call that dumb, wouldn't you?"

"Yes, I would."

"Dumb as a sack full of hammers. It was only a matter of time." He paused for a minute, studied Scotts carefully. He leaned in to her. "You been here before?"

"Yes, Mister Jacob, I have. A couple of times. I knew Lorelei in high school. Not well, I was two grades younger. But she was nice to me and my other friends. She invited us to parties out here."

"Yeah." He seemed to drift off in thought for a moment, then snapped that piercing gaze back to me. "As a matter of fact, tell Adam that for me, will ya? Tell him, 'It was only a matter of time.'"

"About Bobby Rollings getting killed, you mean?"

"Yeah, son, about Bobby Rollings getting killed."

There was the sound of a vehicle coming from the rear of the house. In a moment a dark green pickup swung into view, turned into a gravel parking area near the porch. Lacobee looked over to the driver, raised one finger, then turned back to us.

"Anything else? I got something to take care of."

"We have a few more questions, Mister Jacob," Scotts said, again with that coquettish smile and a small flutter of her eyes. She apparently could be a little minx when she needed to. And it worked.

"Come along, then," he said.

We followed as he got the boy and moved to the truck. They stepped into the passenger side and he laid the rifle across his lap. The driver looked out the window at us. He nodded us toward the bed of the truck. Scotts and I exchanged looks then climbed in back and sat down in the bed. It was littered with crusty dirt and hay.

"Our first hayride!" she said merrily.

Ten minutes of thumps and bumps later we were at a large pond with an open field on the west side and dense tree lines on the north and east sides. The sun was dropping quickly, already showing that "rosy-fingered sky" the poets like to talk about. The two men and the boy got out, both men toting their rifles. The driver also had a long-barrel six-shooter strapped to his hip. They walked toward a fallen tree that seemed set up for an arcade shooting game. We immediately saw why.

On the other side of the pond, just before the tree line, a dozen wild hogs were rooting around, tearing up ground, grunting and groaning like, well, wild hogs.

As we followed them to the fallen tree, Scotts couldn't take her eyes off the driver. He was a big, muscular man with dark brown skin and facial features that defied understanding. Until, that is, Lacobee, called out to him.

"Big Cat, you walk on up that east side of the pond, see if they move when they see you."

That was it: the man had the face of a cat. Black, almond-shaped eyes. A wide, flat nose and narrow jaw. Long, black hair that flared out from the side of his head.

As Big Cat moved away, he chambered a round. Lacobee did the same as we moved over to the tree. He laid his rifle down across it, pointed toward the hogs. He watched Big Cat steal slowly around the pond then turned to us.

"Bastards are tearing up the land," Lacobee explained, mostly to the boy. The boy nodded understanding.

"What do you do about that?" I asked.

"Same you do with any nuisance, get rid of it."

"Do they get into your crops, your cotton and beans?"

"No goddamn beans in my ground! Tears up the land bad as them hogs. No sir. That's all them young ones you hear sayin' that – 'go to soybeans'. Not on my earth."

"So cotton's still king?"

"No it ain't. Sickly crop last year and the year before. Prolly the same this year. Look over there. See that mist over that water? That's cold air doin' that. Winter's staying around longer. Every year, a little longer. Hard to see, hard to feel, but I can tell it. Earth is shifting, too. Moving right out from under our feet. The Bible said it would and it is, sure as God."

Big Cat had moved closer to the hogs, and they began to stir, but without any real direction. Lacobee saw the movement, edged over to the tree and raised his rifle. He took aim at the hog furthest from Cat. He fired a shot and the hog dropped. He fired two more quick rounds, two more dropped. Cat raised his rifle and fired five quick shots, dropping four more. There were only three left, and they were running in circles. Cat started marching right at them, shifted his rifle to his left hand and drew the .45 revolver from his holster. As he closed in, Lacobee fired once more and dropped another. The last two started running right at Cat. He put two shots into the head of each one. They dropped at his feet.

"Like that!" Lacobee said with a grin to the boy. "Like *that,* Bobby!"

"That's some shooting," Scotts said, wowed by the men's speed and marksmanship.

It was impressive. Like you see in the old westerns, only real.

"Been doin' it seventy years, ought to have the hang of it by now," Lacobee said. He stooped over and picked up the spent cartridges, jangled them in his hand a minute and slipped them into his pocket.

He looked up at the sky, saw it growing darker. He waved Cat back to the truck.

He smiled at us. "Cat'll clean up in the morning. He's got a place for the likes of them."

"What do you do with them?" Scotts asked.

"Tell the truth, I don't know for sure. All I know is he takes care of it his ownself." He smiled knowingly. "That's why he's so valuable."

"A man like that is hard to find," I said.

Lacobee eyed me a long moment. I swear I saw a little twinkle come into his eye. He laughed. Then he bent down and told the boy to run ahead and get in the truck. When the boy was in, he turned back to us.

"You two think I did it, don't you? Killed that no count Rollings. Believe them stories that crazy girl of mine's been telling. That right?"

"We wouldn't be the only ones," I said.

"Let's say I did. You think the likes of you are gonna find out? Think that Sheriff of ours can figure it out? You think Adam Manship's gonna work out how I did it?"

"Sounds like you're saying you did."

He shrugged, "What I'm telling you is this: Out here, we take care of things our ownself. We leave all that motion and commotion and emotion to you people uptown. Out here, we get things done."

"Nothing stays a secret forever," I said.

"You wanna bet?" Lacobee grinned. "Ask your boss."

Big Cat fired up the truck and revved the engine. Lacobee gave us both a grunt and then headed to the truck. "You better climb in if you're ridin' back with us."

Cat drove us back to the Big House. He let Scotts and I out at the drive and then pulled up to the house and sat there with the motor running while Lacobee had a word with him.

After a moment, Lacobee got out of the truck and helped the boy step down. He called over to us, "We gotta clean our guns, Cat will take you out." Boy in one hand rifle in the other, he headed to the front steps.

Scotts stood uncertain for a moment then bolted over and stopped in front of him. "Mister Jacob, we're sorry we didn't make the graveside service. We wanted to, but Chief Black told us it was private."

"Did he now? He shouldn't a done that. You'd a been more than welcome. Fact, come back anytime. Come see Lorelei, she'll be glad for the company."

Scotts was taken aback. "Oh. Okay, Mister Jacob. I should do that."

"Yes, you should. That'd be good." He turned to the truck, "Big Cat, take them down to their car."

"We're parked out on the road," Scotts said.

"Out to the road, Cat," he called to him, then looked up at the nearly black sky. "Getting dark. Wouldn't want you two lost out here in all this darkness."

He and the boy headed up the steps. He paused at the top to stomp dirt off his boots. He looked back to me. "You give Adam my regards."

Big Cat stared at us from the truck as he reached across the seat and pushed the passenger door open. Scotts smiled, mouthed a thank you and climbed in. She scooted over beside him. I climbed in next to her.

Scotts tried to start a conversation with Big Cat but he remained silent, kept his big, impassive eyes forward. In a moment, he pulled out of the plantation, onto the road and then up behind her Jeep. I opened the door and stepped out. Scotts hesitated a second, turned and said something quietly to Cat. He looked at her and said nothing. She slid out hastily and slammed the door. He did a U-turn back to the plantation.

"What the hell did you say to him?" I asked as we got in the Jeep.

"Not much. Kinda not much. All I said was, 'We know what happened.'"

"Why would you say something like that?"

"Well, I was hoping for a little more than that blank stare, you know!"

"So Lacobee ordered Rollings killed, Big Cat did the shooting, and you thought maybe he'd confess right there on the spot?"

"Did you see the way they can shoot? Damn! And I thought my daddy was good."

"Rollings was killed with a shotgun at point blank. You don't have to be a good shot to do that."

She said nothing.

"I had no idea you knew this bunch so well," I said.

"Yes you did. I told you I knew Lorelei. It was a long time ago, like—"

There was a sharp sound from deep in the woods. It sounded like a distant gunshot. We rolled down the windows to listen.

"What was that?" Scotts asked.

"Sounded like a shot."

"More hogs?"

"Maybe."

We listened a few minutes and heard nothing more. We continued scanning the woods on both sides of the road. The night was almost black, we could see little to nothing.

"Did you see Lorelei up in the window?" Scotts said in a whisper out of the side of her mouth, eyes still searching the woods.

"No."

"Back at the house. I was standing there with Mister Jacob, just before he went inside. She was upstairs in that dormer window looking down at us."

"Didn't see her."

"She looked weird."

"By weird you mean?"

"I mean she was always weird, but she was looking, like, scary weird."

I hadn't told Scotts about my interview with Lorelei and was about to when she turned on me, waving a finger.

"Look, you're making this way too complicated. Everybody knows he did it. And *he* knows everybody knows it. That's the easy part of this story to understand. The hard part is why you haven't written not one word about this? *The Atlanta Democrat*, our own paper, has run like two paragraphs, while everyone else is giving this half the front page. Why is that?"

I was about to answer when another shot rang out. Then two more, all much closer. We saw quick flashes of light with each loud burst. They were coming from the woods to our left, woods that ran back toward the Big House.

Two more shots ripped into the road right in front of us.

Scotts turned on the headlights and started cranking. The old Jeep fired right up.

Another shot ripped into the road. Then one hit the rear of the Jeep.

"Goddamn!" Scotts said, dropped it into first gear and gassed it. We were just getting up to speed when a figure ran out of the woods, stopped in the middle of the road and started waving at us.

It was Lorelei, standing in our headlights. She was wearing a flowing white nightgown that looked like it'd been ripped and torn. Her hair was a mess, her eyes wide with fear.

She began screaming: "Stop, stop, stop…he's trying to kill me. He's trying to kill me."

She turned back toward the woods she'd come from and lifted a small revolver. She fired one shot then clicked through several empty chambers.

She spun back and looked toward us then collapsed on the road.

Scotts had slammed on the brakes not ten feet from her. She killed the engine, reached under the seat and pulled out a revolver, then jumped out and over to Lorelei. I was right with her.

We rolled Lorelei over. There was the small pistol laying on the asphalt beneath her. She was still breathing. There were no signs of any injuries or wounds.

We turned to the sound of brakes screeching right behind us. It was Big Cat. He flung open the door of his truck and jumped out. He still had the big revolver strapped on his hip.

He hurried over to Lorelei and looked down at her. Then back at us. He saw the gun Scotts was dangling at her side.

He put his hand on his gun and said, "You won't need that." He gave us a long, hard 'back away' stare.

We backed away.

"Thank you," he said in a quiet voice.

There was pain in his other-worldly eyes as he looked down at her.

"Jimsonweed," he said. "She ain't well tonight."

He bent down to lift her off the road. He raised her with ease and cradled her in his arms. As he held her, Lorelei opened her eyes and seemed to regain awareness. She recognized Big Cat and her tortured face relaxed, turned calm. She managed a faint smile at him then closed her eyes again.

Big Cat said nothing more, as if we were no longer there. He bent down with her in his arms and picked up the pistol she'd had. He carried her to the truck and placed her gingerly in the cab. He climbed in and pulled away, headed back to the plantation.

Scotts was trembling head to toe.

"You okay?" I asked.

"Hell no, I'm not okay," she barked. She broke into a big jubilant smile and threw both hands in the air. "I'm great!"

"You're *great?*"

"Hell, yes. Did you see that? Can you believe this?" She paused a second to catch her breath. "My god, that was something! Hey, shouldn't we call the sheriff?"

"Hold on, hold on." I took her arm to anchor her. She seemed about to float away. "Steady now. Tell me what Cat said."

"When? Oh, just then? He said 'jimsonweed.' That's a plant that grows wild out here. It's the country boy's LSD. I guess he meant she was on it. Not a surprise. When we were—"

"Some kind of hallucinogenic?"

"I'll say. When we were in high school. . . ah, never mind. Don't we need to call the sheriff?"

"Let's get back, we can talk about it on the way."

We hustled into the Jeep and pulled out. We rode silently all the way. She was breathing normally by the time we got back to the diner where I'd left my bike.

"We didn't talk about it," she said, "about calling the sheriff."

"We need to do that. Go see him in the morning, tell him what happened. And find out about the shotgun."

"Agreed. Hey, you want to grab a coffee? I am so hyped, I'll never go to sleep."

"I have to get back. Long ride."

She sat still for moment then killed the engine. "Okay, what's with the puzzled look?"

"We can't carry," I said. "So says the Employee Manual."

"Never read it. And whoever wrote it never lived in the country. Besides, I don't *carry* a gun, I *have* a gun. I just keep it handy."

"Very handy."

"My daddy says, 'Teach a girl to shoot, she'll never have to file a restraining order.'"

"You know how to use it?"

"Hell yes. Anyway, it's part of the package, so either live with the stupid *Employee Manual* violation or fire me." She gave me a sour look and turned away, stared across the dark diner parking lot for a moment.

"Look, it was a condition of going back to work for you. From Travis. And you see why don't you? Now I've got a damn bullet hole in the back of my car I have to explain. You see why?"

I had to admit, I saw why.

"That's the deal," she said. "I've got no choice. Plus, I actually do know how to use it. I know you were like a Marine or something, but I can probably outshoot you, if you ever want a contest."

She smiled and waited for me to decide something.

I pulled out my wallet. "Here. Here's your first week's pay. Three hundred bucks, plus a hundred bonus."

"Really? Now *that's* cool! Four hundred smackers! Including a *hazardous duty* bonus!"

"Right."

She looked at me with a tart grin. "Shoot, with the tits working and the bonus bucks, Travis'll be all in for sure. Bullet hole or not."

I smiled and sent her on her merry way.

After a moment of standing there, looking up into the black, starless sky, I fired up the Triumph and headed back to Atlanta. I was glad I'd ridden it down that morning. The trip back, in the dark, in the silence, in the hum and rumble of the little black machine that bore me along would be welcome. It'd give me time to consider. To consider what all I had to report to Mr. Manship.

29

I woke the next morning to an empty bed and a pounding head. Lacey had been waiting at my place the night before with a bottle of Tiger 186, the world's cheapest wine at less than a buck a bottle. She called it a party favor and dared me to drink even one glass. I took the dare and did her one better – I drank the whole bottle.

I don't know what we did after that, but from the aching in every joint it must have been strenuous. A salacious note beside my coffee pot recounted our night, promised she'd be back for more, and reminded me that she'd left for an early flight to New Orleans. She'd be there two weeks – a week of training then a week-long national lawyer conference.

To get that corky taste of cheap wine out of my mouth I drank a pot of thick, black coffee. I worked on bringing my notes up to date. On complex stories like this, I usually made a "know/don't know" ledger. The "don't know" side on this one was full. The "know" side was lacking.

I also fielded a call from Mrs. Christian cancelling my meeting that evening with Mr. Manship.

"He will be away a short while and I will call to reschedule when he returns," she offered. I had the urge to ask when he might return but resisted. Mrs. Christian did not strike me as one prone to speculation.

I spent much of the afternoon tinkering with the bike. I'd noticed it running a little ragged the day before. It was time for an oil change, valve check and carburetor cleaning.

Done with that, I took it for a road test by running down to the newspaper to see my old boss, Calvin Daniels, about some of my "don't knows."

Daniels had fallen from grace over the last several years, owing at least in part to his longstanding affair with ol' John Barleycorn. At one time he'd been a top editor at the *Democrat*. Stuck on the weekend desk now, he still knew where all the bodies in Georgia were buried – and for the most part, who'd buried them.

"Check your damn messages," Daniels said as I stuck my head in his office. "That woman's called half a dozen times today, she's driving us crazy down here."

In my box were a handful of pink messages. Half of them were from Lorelei Rollings, taken within the last three hours. They all bore the same message: "Urgent, call ASAP."

I called. Mrs. Rollings answered with bubbly enthusiasm and said she sincerely appreciated my returning her call. She wanted to apologize for her terrible behavior the other day. She had been, of course, grief stricken, and while that was no excuse for her conduct, it was an explanation she hoped I would accept. She also wanted to invite me to coffee at her Atlanta townhouse. She had, she said, important information for the story I was doing on her husband. She would like to give that information to me personally. She made no mention of her jimsonweed frenzy the night before.

We set a meeting for the next morning then I drifted back to Daniels' office.

"What the hell, Coates, you joined a babe-of-the-month club?" he asked with a dry grin.

"The story I'm on, the Rollings killing."

"How's that going? Oh yeah, before I forget, the City Ed tells me you're off his PITA List for now – that's Pain In The Ass in case you forgot. He was getting fed up with you, but now that he never sees you, he thinks he likes you. There's a moral there somewhere, but who gives a shit. Tell me about the story."

I took a seat and was about to dive in when his phone rang. He held up a finger to shush me then answered. After a minute he put the call on hold.

"I gotta take this, Coates. You want to grab a beer tonight when I get off, tell me about it?"

"Yeah, I would. Drigger's place?"

"You bet. I'm done here at nine, be there by nine-thirty or so. Bring plenty of cash, these are on you."

I left the newspaper and rode the bike around town for another hour. While my rides were often simply for the joy of riding, this one wasn't. I had picked up a tail again, and while it looked like an unmarked cop car, the driver wasn't Weaver this time.

I wondered who it was and decided to find out. As long as I stayed downtown, I knew I could lose him. I had an edge: maneuverability on the bike, knowledge of the alleys and one-way streets, low visibility. It didn't take long to shake the tail, circle around behind him and end up the pursuer rather than the pursued.

At a stop light I pulled alongside the car, flipped the visor on my helmet and looked at the driver. He refused to look my way. It didn't matter. He knew I was right there, and he knew I knew he was tailing me. He also knew I recognized him: It was Boyd O'Con, the Latham County Sheriff's dispatcher I'd talked to a few days back. Scotts' cousin.

When the light changed, I gunned it, took a hard left, then zipped down the first service alley I came to. Boyd O'Con wouldn't be seeing me again, not that evening anyway.

30

DRIGGER's Bar and Grill sat a half-dozen miles east of the Atlanta city limits, past the suburbs and well beyond the proposed new interstate loop. Few knew about the joint, and it was almost impossible to get to. The only thing that kept it afloat was the fact that Drigger himself was the only employee and, since he lived there in a back room, kept it open 24-7.

It made the perfect spot for under-the-radar meetings, which is how several of us at the *Democrat* used it. Unhappily for Drigger, we kept the place secret.

I pulled into the small lot at the rear about 9:45 that night. There was Calvin Daniels' car and three others.

Inside, some country tune was drifting through the pewter haze. Daniels sat in a dim-lit booth in a far corner. He glanced up, shot me with his finger gun and lifted his beer. He focused hard on the beer. He could do that well, focus. He was a good drinker, too – his bottle was drained by the time I got to the table.

"I wasn't going to wait on your ass," he said, looking up and handing me the empty. "While you're up, grab us a couple. Each."

I went over to the bar and gave it a bare-knuckle rap – the house call to place an order. Drigger stumbled wearily out of the kitchen and eyed me. I held up four fingers and he turned and plodded toward the cooler.

There were only four other people in the place, three young guys and a woman in a shiny dress who looked old enough to be their mother. They were huddled in a dark corner on the other side of the pool tables. She was getting the boys' undivided attention.

Drigger put four longnecks up on the bar and started to pry one with his opener. I stopped him.

"That's okay, Drigger. We bite 'em off." I put ten bucks on the bar and took the beers.

"Yeah, tough guys, you two," he said with a wave of his dish towel and turned away.

When I got back to the table, Daniels was watching the quartet in the far corner. The woman in the shiny dress sat with her elbows on the table, leaned in, facing two of the boys. The third boy was nuzzled next to her and under the table had his hand shoved up her dress. She was alternately laughing and groaning sweetly. One of the boys across the table leaned in and kissed her lips. The boy beside her slipped his other hand inside her blouse.

"Must be a family affair, all that love in the room," Daniels said as he grabbed two beers. He popped one open with his key ring and passed it to me, then opened his own.

"To you and your love life," he said and tipped my bottle.

"And to yours, wherever it is."

"Right here in my hand, man, right here in my hand."

He quickly finished that one, slid it aside and reached across the table for my unopened beer.

"Hey, hold up, you still have one right there," I protested.

"I know I told you *three*, Coates. If you don't want to listen, that's your problem."

"Yeah, right." I lit a cigarette.

"So," he said, halfway into my beer, "you looked a little troubled when you came into the paper today."

"Did I?"

"Yep."

"How much do you know, Calvin?"

"Not much. I know Manship called me on the desk last Sunday, told me to send *you specifically* to New Bethany, and to keep it on the down low. The next day you were pulled off the roster, moved to Special Assignment, and we get orders to give the Rollings murder no play at all. That's it."

"That's it?"

"Oh, yeah…and the guy handling the story – that'd be you – has been looking puzzled lately. Now. There. That's it."

"I'm not sure how much I can tell you."

"You don't need to tell me anything. Just ask. If I can help, I will. You know what they say, you'll never get a kiss winking in the dark." He grinned and nodded toward the quartet, "Like those boys over there."

The boys over there looked to be headed for more than kisses. And it was, indeed, interesting to watch. But at the moment I wanted answers more than soft-core entertainment.

"Okay. Nagging question – and I doubt you have an answer, but here goes: Why is Manship following this story? Personally? Why this special interest, this off-the-books investigation? On the surface this Rollings murder may look like some blood simple killing, but I think there's more to it. What's the boss after?"

"You're right, I can't answer that."

"Already, more help than I could have imagined."

"But you just did."

"I did? What was my answer?" I asked.

"Personally."

"What?"

"You asked why he's following this story *personally*?"

"I did."

"That's the answer, dumb ass. It's *personal*."

Oh. Yeah.

"Look, Coates, let me give you some advice. *It's none of your goddamn business.* This is your boss. He pays you – all of us – damn well. And he's asked you to do something for him. If he wants you to know why, he'll tell you. Meanwhile, do the job."

Oh. Yeah.

"So, what are the questions you need answered for the story?" he asked and took a big swig from his third beer. "Shoot."

"Yeah, okay. Do you know of any local, state or federal investigation into Georgia Commerce Bank?"

"No," he said and took out a note pad, started jotting, "but I can find out for you."

"You know who Jacob Lacobee is?"

Daniels nodded. "Who doesn't? Big cotton farmer. Big money. Connected. Very well connected – state, even national, I hear."

"Had you ever heard of Bobby Rollings before he was murdered?"

"Yeah."

"And?"

"In Atlanta he was a player, but not a major leaguer – not yet anyhow. He was still a comer. Word is the old man, Lacobee, hooked him up financially. You know the story: Connections, connections, connections."

"I do know that story. Did you know Hooper – Gary Hooper?"

"I did. *Wall Street Journal* guy, now. Worked here about fifteen years ago. First black man to work Metro for us. Manship hired him personally. That was a helluva good idea, too, given we're in Atlanta, Georgia. Hooper turned out to be some kind of newshound. He could get to shit no one else could get to. Made connections fast. Fact, I hear he's still tight with black leaders here, including our mayor, Mr. Young. Straight shooter as far as I know."

Daniels took a break for half a beer, then went on.

"Come to think of it, he went off the books once in a while, just like you are now. I forgot about that. Years ago, before he went to *The Journal*."

"Is that a fact?"

"I don't make shit up. How do you know Hooper?"

"I met him recently."

Calvin eyed me carefully and took another swig. "Yeah? Small world ain't it? So what else is troubling you?"

"I'm being followed."

He looked around the empty room. "Yeah, I can tell. The place is crawling with subversives."

"Seriously."

"You probably are. Lot of our guys are, or have been. Not uncommon. Been going on for years. Mostly our competitors, trying to figure out what we're digging into."

"I think it's the cops from Latham County."

He shrugged. "Could be. Cops ain't always the angels, you know."

"I did know that."

"Speaking of angels, you still tappin' that lovely in the DA's office, what's-her-name...Lacey something?"

"We're dating."

"That what it is?"

"What do you think it is?"

"I think it's something you need to look out for. She may be a helluva source for you. Fine tail, too, from the looks of her. And all that's fine and dandy. But that could be a dangerous one."

"Why would you call her dangerous?"

He considered it a minute. "Cause she's a fuckin' woman!"

Calvin whooped at his own joke loud enough to draw Drigger's attention. He shot us a questioning look from behind the bar. I held up four fingers and he nodded, headed for the cooler.

"I'm going for more beers," I told Daniels. "Save my seat."

He let out another big laugh.

Across the room, the woman in the shiny dress let out a big, hot, steamy sigh and moaned with pleasure, "Ohhhhh, you bastard. . . ohhhh. . . don't stop now, don't you dare…Ohhhh!"

Her honesty and sincerity were without question.

When I got back to the table with the beers, Calvin and I hoisted one to honesty. And another to sincerity. And so on until we were out of virtues to salute.

31

I was at Lorelei Rollings' townhouse the next morning at ten. She threw open the door with a grand flair.

"Come in, come in, come in, Mr. Coates!"

She wore a broad smile and a slinky satin dress cut low in the front and lower in the back. She must have been headed to a cocktail party right after our meeting.

She apologized once again for her previous behavior as she guided me through the house to a spacious sitting room. For the chic modern townhouse it was, located in the chi-chi part of town, it had an old world look inside. But it was finely done-up, as they say here in the South. Either Lorelei Rollings had exquisite taste in interior design and décor, or she had a very expensive decorator. My bet was on the latter.

"Please make yourself comfortable. I'll get you a…coffee? Or shall we try something stronger?"

"Coffee will be good."

She'd been gone from the room no more than a couple of minutes when her son wandered in. He appeared in a daze and was holding a bloody rag to his face. He had what looked like a recent bruise on the left side of his forehead. He apparently wasn't expecting anyone to be in the room. When he saw me he leapt back, fell against a glass-fronted curio cabinet and rattled the contents.

"Jesus Christ, Robert," Mrs. Rollings shouted as she hurried back into the room. She quickly sat my coffee in front of me then snatched him by the arm and pulled him from the room.

She hissed as she marched him off. "I told you to stay in your own goddamn room, Robert. Get in there and stay in there."

After a moment, she returned and settled into a chair opposite me. A warm smile came to her face as she folded her hands in her lap – a simple enough act which seemed practiced for effect. The effect being to pull the already low cut front of her dress even lower.

"I am so sorry. Robert has been having a difficult time since his father…well, you can imagine if you'd seen your father killed before your very eyes."

"That must have been awful for him."

"Yes, it was. It was. Awful for us all."

Her face turned grave. She looked at me with piercing blue eyes – those same piercing blue eyes her grandfather had.

"I seem to be always apologizing to you," she said.

"No need. It's understandable given what you've been through."

"Do you have that little recorder thing?"

"Yes ma'am."

"You may put it on the table and turn it on."

I did. She watched with vague curiosity.

"There," I said with a smile. "Open and above board."

She allowed herself a modest smile.

"You said you have important information for me?" I said.

"Yes. I wanted to tell you…I was…not myself the other day. I accused my grandfather of something I know he couldn't do, he *didn't* do."

"And that was kill your husband?"

"He did *not* do that. My grandfather did *not* do that."

"And you know that to be true?"

"Yes. My husband was…he had enemies…he was…not who he seemed to be."

She looked away, then cast her eyes downward. She began to study the dress she wore. She seemed entranced by it. She brushed at the satin lightly with the back of her hand, as if to smooth out a crease. She looked intensely at the fabric of the dress.

"This has more purple in it than I thought. What do you think?"

"I'm sorry, I'm not sure what you're asking."

"This dress. Would you say it is purple, or is it black?"

"Oh, I see. It looks more purple I guess. But I'm not very good with colors."

"I thought it was black when I put it on. I should go change." She stood up to leave.

"Oh no, ma'am. You don't need to go change for me."

She spun and looked at me. "I wasn't going to change for you. For Bobby. My husband. He's dead, you know. Out of respect, I should be in black. In mourning. In black."

As she turned to leave, the boy came running into the room. He still held the bloody cloth to his face. He was screaming.

"I want to go to Papa's! I want to go to Papa's!"

She slapped at him but missed. "Shut up, Robert, and go back to your room. I have to go change this dress."

She reached down to grab him. He darted away from her and once again slammed into the curio cabinet. "I want to go to Papa's!"

He bounded away from the cabinet and ran behind the chair I sat in, putting me between him and his mother.

"Robert, you little shit. Come here right now." She came charging at him.

I stood up, stopping her.

"Mrs. Rollings, please. The boy seems genuinely upset."

"You? What would you know about upset? You get out of here right now."

I felt the boy grab my leg and cling to it.

She stopped and glared at him, then erupted. "Both of you, get out of here right now."

"Yes ma'am," I said. I turned to the boy and took his arm. I pulled him closer to my side. "If it's okay with you, Mrs. Rollings, I'll take the boy down to the plantation for you. That's where he wants to go, right? That's his Papa?"

She moved in close to me, so close I could feel her breath on my face. She began rubbing her warm hand on my crotch. Her eyes danced with flirtation, with invitations to taboos.

She put her lips on mine and whispered, "Take him. I don't care. He's not mine anyway."

I pulled away from her, grabbed my recorder from the table and began to tug the boy out of the room. She stepped in front of me and again put her face in mine. She pressed her breast to my chest and began to stroke me again. She blew her warm breath into my lips.

"After you take him, come back," she whispered. "We'll finish our visit."

She slowly ran her tongue over my lips then stepped aside.

32

THE boy began settling down the minute we got out the door. We hurried down the street and around the corner to where I'd parked. Luckily, there was no one on the street to witness a man yanking along a small, teary-eyed boy holding a bloody rag to his face. That wouldn't have gone well.

I didn't discount the possibility that the boy's crazy mother might call the cops and say I'd kidnapped her son. I was pretty sure, though, I'd gotten enough on tape to protect myself against a claim like that.

We got to my parking spot and there was my bike, right where I'd left it. In my haste to get the boy out of the house, I'd forgotten I was on the motorcycle. Normally, riding two-up on the bike was not a problem for me – Lacey often enjoyed a spin around the city on the back. But a five-year old who was already scared out of his wits might be a challenge.

I crouched down to the boy, eye-to-eye, and held his shoulders.

"Okay, Robert. My name is Gil. Can you say that?"

He looked at me a moment then lowered the bloody rag from his face and nodded.

"Say it, then. Say 'Gil.'"

"Gil."

"Okay, good. Now let me take a look at you. Are you hurt?"

He shook his head and held out the rag. There were no noticeable marks anywhere, except the bruise on his forehead. It looked like he'd had a nosebleed – undoubtedly from his mother's hand. The bleeding had stopped, so I took the rag.

"I'm going to take you to Papa's. Would you like to go to Papa's?"

He nodded.

"Good. Okay. We're going to your Papa's. First, we need to go get my car. Would you like to go for a short motorcycle ride? On that motorcycle right there? On the back?"

He looked at me, then looked at the bike. A small smile crept across his face. The smile grew wider as he turned back.

"How's that sound? Want to ride?"

His little smile turned into a big "Yes."

The kid had an angelic face. He had blue eyes like his mother's, only softer, warmer. And a gentle smile. I put my helmet on him and pulled it as snug as I could without choking him. It was loose and wobbly but better than nothing.

"There, we're ready. Let's get on and go. It's not far. We'll be breaking every law in the land, but who cares, huh? They get after us, we'll outrun them."

The boy wrapped his arms around me and held on tight as we pulled away. I couldn't see his face but would have bet money he was wearing a grin a mile wide, like any kid on the back of a motorcycle.

33

JACOB Lacobee couldn't have been more appreciative.

The boy had jumped out of my car and run across the field to his tractor the minute he'd spotted him. He'd nearly knocked the old man down jumping in his arms – a Labrador retriever finding his long lost master.

"Thank you," Lacobee said to me, standing with the boy in his arms at my car. "That mother of his never did know how to handle him."

"He seems okay," I said. I handed him the bloody rag the boy had been holding to his face. "Had a nosebleed, maybe."

"Looks it," Lacobee said, frowning, looking closely again at the boy's face, pushing his hair back away from his forehead. "Got himself a bump there, too."

"I was interviewing Mrs. Rollings, he kept saying he wanted to go to Papa's, so I offered to bring him down. She said okay."

"Oh yeah? That the way it went?"

"More or less."

"Prolly *less* be my bet," Lacobee said.

He put the boy down and spoke to him gently. "You run inside and get a cold drink from Mamaw. I gotta thank the man for bringing you home."

The boy nodded and raced up the front steps.

Lacobee watched him go then turned back and considered me carefully. "Like I say, thank you for bringing him home."

"Looks like he's glad to be here."

"Damn sure is. This is home, and he knows it."

"But his father didn't agree? What they say is you and his father didn't agree on that."

"Me and his father didn't agree on much a nothing. But that's none of your business. The man's dead now, so even if it was true, it don't matter does it?"

"You're right."

"I am most times." He grinned and started away, then turned back, cocked his head. "Your newspaper sure don't think this killing is very important business, I reckon."

"How's that?"

"You don't print hardly a word about it. You can tell Adam Manship I'm personally offended by that."

"I will tell him. I believe you said you and Mr. Manship are friends? Or acquaintances?"

"Did I say that?"

"You implied it when we spoke with you before."

"Did I, now? When you and that girl was out here right after the funeral? I'll be dern, I must be touched." He grinned and tapped his temple. "That was only a couple days back and already I don't remember saying it."

"I believe you did."

He laughed and patted himself on the stomach. "Guess I did then, if you remember it so well." He paused for a second then leveled his gaze.

"Me and Adam go back a ways. We sure do." He chuckled to himself. "You know, you need to tell Adam to come out here his ownself some time. Not send some hired hand. Matter of fact, I owe him a dove hunt, so tell him he needs to come on out and let me make good on that."

"I'll tell him."

"You do that." He gave me a solemn gaze, presumably to insure I remembered his message. Then he added, "Thanks again."

I watched him walk back out across the field to his tractor. He climbed on, fired it up and was stirring up dust in no time. He was a stand-and-deliver man, that much was clear. Rock solid. And the boy must have felt that solidity, that security, the way he clung to him. The old man was the kid's anchor, for better or worse. I began to understand what Lorelei meant when she said, "He's not mine, anyway." That kid belonged to the old man, pure and simple. And she, Lorelei Rollings, seemed caught in a wicked double bind she was unlikely to ever escape – the twin bindings of her own ruinous impulses and an unyielding lord and master.

34

I left the plantation and turned toward New Bethany. I hadn't planned to be down here today, but since I was, thought it a good time to check in with Scotts. She was supposed to have learned more about the shotgun. And I was curious to hear how she'd sold the bullet hole in the Jeep to her husband.

I wasn't two miles down the road when I saw the tail. This one was a little different from the others – a small orange motorcycle that was struggling to keep up with me even at 50 miles per hour. In a second I recognized the long strands of blond hair flapping out the sides of the helmet.

I pulled to the side of the road and waited for it to catch up. It sputtered to a jerky stop behind me. I hopped out of the car and walked back.

"What the hell is *this*?" I said to Scotts as she sat astride the bike tugging her helmet off.

"Backup transportation," she said with a big smile and sweeping gesture. "You know, in case, like, my car gets all shot to pieces or something."

"You're kidding."

"No, I'm not. Pretty cool, huh? I borrowed it from my dad. It's a Honda Trail 90, and he uses it for hunting because his old legs won't carry him to his deer stand any more. He has to ride this.

Only deer season is over for now, so he's letting me learn to ride. What d'ya think?"

"What the hell are you doing out here? – that's what I think."

"I told you, I'm learning to ride. Oh, and something else. You see how small this is? I can go anywhere and never be seen. Perfect surveillance vehicle."

"It's bright orange."

"Well, true. I already told Travis I needed one of my own so I don't have to borrow Dad's. I'll get one that blends better."

"I'm asking again, what are you doing here? You forget two nights ago someone shooting at us? Right here?"

"I could ask you the same thing. Anyhow, that was just Lorelei and she was all screwed up on something. She didn't know what she was doing. That wasn't anything. Anyhow, I was checking out some back roads, in case we need to keep an eye on the place."

"You don't need to worry about that."

"I'm not *worrying* about it, just considering it. For instance…is there a way to get from the plantation over to the Rollings home, and then back, without getting out on the highway? Is there? Do you know?"

"No, I don't."

"I do. And there is. Or, do you know where that family plot is – that cemetery they call DeRussey?"

"No."

"I do. And I'll bet you don't know that Will Black now knows who owned the shotgun that killed Bobby R."

"Bobby R.?"

"Bobby Rollings, you know who I mean."

"I know his wife is a madwoman."

"Like the Madwoman of Chaillot? Like that? With Katherine Hepburn? You know we saw that movie not too long ago. Travis and I rented it at the video store."

"A different madness."

"Oooooh! So, you saw her? You saw Lorelei?" She beamed. "Let's go. Follow me into town, we'll grab coffee and swap notes."

I glanced at my watch. It was later than I thought.

"Can't do it. I have a meeting with the boss this evening and need to get back to Atlanta. How about this instead—"

"Hey, who is your boss, anyway? If you're my boss, then I'm working for your boss, too, right? I ought to know that, don't you think? I mean, say something were to happen to you, god forbid. Who would I report to?"

"My boss is…you don't know him. He's not. . . I can't tell you right now. Maybe later."

"Oh, shit, now this *is* getting weird. I like it!"

"Good, then you'll love this: How about a secret meeting in a sleazy bar. Noon tomorrow, in Atlanta, on the east side."

I wrote down the address and phone number for Drigger's place and stuck it in her jacket pocket.

"Oke doke," she said with a smile a click and a wink. "See you there, boss."

She pulled her helmet back on, snapped it, started up the trail bike and whirled away. For a beginner she handled it well. If her over-confidence didn't overcome her common sense, she might survive.

35

I was at Mr. Manship's promptly at nine that evening. Mrs. Christian ushered me into his office right away.

He stood facing a large floor easel, cupping his chin in his hand and studying a painting that sat on the easel. He wore a rich navy suit, a dark tie and still had on the white Borsalino Fedora he always wore in public. It was not a stylish hat for the day, but after speaking to Mr. Manship for even a few minutes, you had to agree *this hat* fit him perfectly, regardless of fashion.

He waved me over to the painting.

"Tell me what you see here, Mr. Coates," he said with a gesture to the picture.

I looked at it. "A can of soup."

He nodded, glanced at the painting, and then back to me. "Look closer. Take your time."

I studied it carefully. Okay, it wasn't a can of soup.

"It's a box of soup mix. Onion soup. Campbell's. A painting of a box of Campbell's Soup mix."

"Anything else?"

"It's signed by Andy Warhol. The pop artist. He died recently, didn't he?"

"Last year, 1987. Anything else?"

"If he died last year, this was signed the year he died."

"It was."

"And, he was famous for soup cans, but this is not a soup can, it's a box of soup. The next generation soup? Soup in a box? Instant soup? I don't know. . . is it symbolic of something?"

Mr. Manship lifted his hands slightly and shrugged. "Maybe. But it's the only soup-in-a-box he ever painted."

He studied the picture a moment more then removed his hat and placed it on a hat rack. He took his usual chair. He patted his hands on the arms of the chair as he sat and took a couple of deep breaths.

"You just acquired it?" I asked.

"Yesterday. In New York."

"As an investment or because you have a passion for it?"

"Very astute question. Some of both, I'd say. And," he added as he smiled and waved his hand toward his walls full of paintings, "I've grown tired of nothing but these old men hanging around."

Mrs. Christian tapped on the door and stepped in to tell him that she would be leaving for the evening if there was nothing else. But, she added, she would be happy to stay longer if he needed her, that would not be a problem.

He told her she should be on her way. With a trace of a smile he offered her safe travels.

Once she left the room, he chuckled and shook his head. "She lives one floor below. I don't require that of her, but she imagines I might come unraveled were she not always close at hand."

We sat for a moment. He took a sip from a glass of cold tea Mrs. Christian had left on his side table. "How is our inquiry?"

"I'm being tailed," I said. "All the way over here just now, and a half dozen times in the past week."

He showed mild amusement. "That's good. We wouldn't be doing our jobs if you weren't."

"That's what Calvin Daniels said."

"He's right. Listen to him, he's a good man."

"I think it's the Chief Deputy from Latham County, Will Black. Some of his men."

"Are you concerned?"

"I've never been tailed before. Not that I know of."

"I'll bet you have, you just haven't noticed it until now."

He offered me a cigar. I declined. He lit one for himself.

"How is our new girl working out?"

"She's very good. She's resourceful, forthright and gutsy. At the same time, she has a lightness verging on gaiety."

"Sounds like someone nice to be around. I'd like to meet her."

"Yes, sir."

He took a draw on his cigar then sat it in the tray beside him. "These are interesting people down in Latham County, would you say?"

"Yes, they are."

"Not your run-of-the-mill story?"

"There's the murder and probably some corruption in there somewhere – it would be a surprise if there weren't – but I don't think either is the lead."

"What *do* you think is the lead?"

"I don't know, yet. I think it's more about tangled loyalties and twisted hearts."

He tipped a finger toward me. "Very nice. I like that – 'tangled loyalties and twisted hearts.' Give me a for instance."

"For one, it's the wife. Lorelei Rollings. I can't put my finger on it yet, sir, but there's something tragic about her. At the same time, it feels like she's so innocent, so naïve, or something. Lost in love, maybe."

"Nothing stirs my soul like the smell of hearts on fire."

"There is a fire there, yes, sir."

"And your tangled loyalties?"

"Yes, sir. Well, I've met with Jacob Lacobee twice, and both times he has referred to a long-time relationship you and he have."

"Yes. We both sit on the board at Georgia Commerce Bank, as you know."

"The bank Bobby Rollings worked for," I added.

"Yes."

"Both of whom – the bank and Mr. Rollings – are being investigated by the DOJ."

"According to Mr. Hooper," he reminded me.

"Right, sir. According to Hooper. But Lacobee seemed to be suggesting a relationship much more than that. Beyond that."

"I see," Mr. Manship took a long sip of his iced tea. "And so you are wondering how Jacob Lacobee might tie in to this inquiry I have you on – apart from possibly killing Mr. Rollings?"

"Yes, sir, it has crossed my mind."

He looked down at his cigar and saw it had gone out. He took a moment to light it and then drew a few puffs.

"The thing about a question like that," he continued, "is it leads to more questions. And those, in their turn, to even more questions. More, bigger, better questions. That's the important part. Good questions are far more important than their answers. Ask any doctor, ask any scientist. Even the philosophers, the theologians. They'll all tell you the same: A good question beats a good answer any day. "So, if I gave you the answers—or whatever answers I might have—then you might be inclined to stop asking questions."

"Yes, sir."

"But let me tell you this, because I doubt you would learn it otherwise: I had a brother, Louis – an older brother by eight years. He was much smarter than I and ten times the human being. He should be running this company instead of me. But he was killed when he was sixteen. This was long ago, in 1932. He was shot dead, through the heart, left floating in a creek behind our farm. I found him."

He again paused for a sip of tea, then went on.

"You asked if Jacob Lacobee and I are acquainted. We are. But we are not what you would call friends. It was he and my brother, Louis – they were the friends."

He fell silent.

After a moment I asked, "Did they ever find out—"

"No one knows who shot him."

He said no more. In time he stood and extended his hand.

"A reporter lives in that penumbra between fact and fantasy, Mr. Coates. How you sort it out decides the story you tell. That's the difficult part, isn't it?"

"Yes, sir, it is."

"Thank you for the report. I will have Mrs. Christian arrange for you and Mrs. Scott to join me for dinner one evening at the club. I'm looking forward to meeting her."

36

SIDEBAR:
"Memo to Demos: Get Organized"

Excerpt: *The Atlanta Democrat, April 22, 1988*
From an editorial by Adam Manship, Publisher

The 1988 Democratic National Convention comes to The Omni in Atlanta this summer.

Will Rogers famously said, "I don't belong to any organized political party; I'm a Democrat." He died in 1935 and almost certainly wasn't anticipating the Democratic Party of today – the party about to throw its big shindig right here in our town.

But he seems to have presaged it. This party is a mess, and that reality can be reflected no better than in its plans for this convention – plans released to the press just two days ago.

Get this: Organizers for the convention have chosen pastel colors for the backgrounds in the belief they'll play better on television. Play better than what? They're going with the colors salmon, azure and eggshell, instead of the traditional red, white and blue. If you're a Democrat, does waving a flag of salmon, azure and eggshell make you feel better about your party?

No, we didn't think so.

Next, consider the slate of speakers, a tired list of fire-brands, fogies and no-names with not a coherent voice among them: Ted Kennedy, Jesse Jackson, Jimmy Carter, Walter Mondale, George McGovern and some kid named Bill Clinton. Does that list make you want to stay up until midnight every night for a week so you can hear all the good ideas the Demos have about your future?

Right, that's what we figured.

And how about the candidates in this stable? Michael Dukakis, Jesse Jackson, Richard Stallings, Lloyd Bentsen, Joe Biden, and Dick Gephardt, to name the ones who assure us they still have enough nerve to stand up and talk on national television in front of a fruit-pop flag.

This is more than just the disparate face of a party; this is a party in total disarray, mentally and emotionally.

There are no "old order" Democrats here, no "new order" Demos either. And nothing, we can see, in between or above or beyond. We expect the worst for them, whoever the top two on the ticket are.

It wasn't that long ago – 1972, in fact – that the Democrats sent Mr. McGovern off to perhaps the worst defeat in presidential election history. Don't be surprised if history doesn't repeat itself this fall.

37

Scotts was supposed to meet me at noon at Drigger's. She came stomping into the joint an hour late. She wore a troubled look. Her brow was crimped and wrinkled and her lips were pinched together in a thin red line of bother. She plopped her big tote bag on the table and noisily took a chair.

"You have trouble finding the place?" I asked and glanced at my watch.

"I am being followed." she said, her face reddening. "All the way up here. By my own damn cousin, Boyd O'Con. He was wearing these ridiculous dark glasses and some stupid cap but I'd know that boxy little head of his anywhere."

"You try to lose him?"

She ignored the question. "He was in a cop car for god's sake! How obvious is that?"

"So you're pissed?"

"Well, yeah. My first time, and it's with my *cousin!*"

"Are you aware of what you just said?"

"What?" She pulled her chin back and scrunched her eyebrows. "Oh. Yeah."

"I know what you meant. And welcome to the club. Do you want something to eat or drink?"

"No thanks, not hungry or thirsty. You, too?"

"Me, too, what?"

"You're being followed, too, for god's sake! How can you forget what we were talking about two seconds ago? Jeeez."

"Yes, me, too. Step over to the door and check it out. There'll be two of them out there now – your cousin, and one of Will Black's other boys in a brown sedan."

"We must be onto something."

"Could be, but that's not what the tail's about."

"What do you mean?"

"The tails are Will Black keeping an eye on us, protecting us. It all adds up: the warnings he's given us; the fact that Mr. Manship just smiled last night when I told him I was being followed; the fact that Mr. Manship knew about the killing so damn fast. Will Black called him, it had to be him. Will Black sent you to pick me up. It's all right there in front of us. Will Black and Manship are connected somehow. That's what I mean."

"Whoa! You work for Adam Manship? The owner of our paper and about a billion others, *that* Mr. Manship?"

"That's right. It's a special assignment – we're something like his personal investigative unit for this story."

"Like the CIA?"

"I wouldn't go *that* far."

"Damn, this *is* cool! Hey, weren't you an investigator in the Army or something?"

"No. A correspondent. And it was the Marines."

"But you were in the war, in Vietnam? Is that where you got that scar? – which looks kinda cool, by the way."

"That's a secret."

Scotts' eyes widened a moment then she began a noticeable effort to gather herself, to rein in her freewheeling excitement. She sat up straight and pulled on her sober face. "So, we're on, like, a secret mission?"

"Yes," I said in a whisper. "Very hush-hush. Top secret." I leaned in close. "I sought ve'd gone ofer all zis, Natasha."

"Are you mocking me?"

"Maybe a little. But look, Mr. Manship wants to meet you."

"Really?"

"Really."

"Oh, damn."

"It will be fine, don't worry."

"Don't worry?" she said.

"Don't worry. And you're repeating me. Did you know you do that sometimes?"

"Did I know I do what sometimes?"

"Very funny. Back to why we're here," I said.

"Okay. Wait a minute. Back up. You think Will Black is protecting us? From, like, evil or something?"

"Correct."

"You're sure?"

"That's what I think."

She stared at me a moment without blinking. She threw one hand up to halt the conversation then rose slowly and crept over to the side door. She squeaked it open and took a peek into the parking lot. She eased the door closed and casually returned to the table. She sat down but could no longer contain her delight.

"You were right! Two of them! I started to wave at Boyd, but didn't."

"That was a good idea."

"But this is a good thing. We've got somebody covering us. I mean, we did get shot at, you know. So, I can reassure Travis, tell him I'm covered. Right?"

"You tell me. If somebody thinks we need protecting, the question is: From what?"

"Oh, yeah," she said, slowly leaning back in her chair, biting her lip. "Bummer."

I let her stew on that a minute while I stepped over to the bar and got Drigger to pour me another cup of coffee. He filled it up and gave me a sideways grin.

"Finally, you bring somebody decent to look at," he said. "Must be your sister."

"Close, Drigger. A colleague."

"Lucky you. My colleague was my wife. Lucky me, she hated this place and left five years ago."

"She didn't like this joint? I can't imagine that." I put two bucks on the bar and went back to the table.

Scotts was furiously scribbling notes, impervious to anything outside the borders of her notepad. I sipped on my coffee and watched her. She was actually a very attractive woman. Despite her paler-than-normal skin and the rubier-than-red lipstick, her angular facial features gave her a strong, classic look. Her eyes were deep blue-green, and when she did manage to hold them still on you for any length of time, were penetrating. I'd watched her give that penetrating look to Jacob Lacobee and even he had been momentarily mesmerized.

"I got it," she said, looking up from her notes and waving her pencil at me. "But first, you said you saw Lorelei. Tell me."

I gave her the account of both meetings with Lorelei Rollings, and of taking the boy down to his grandfather. She listened intently then shook her head.

"I knew she was crazy," Scotts said. "Everybody in high school said she was. I thought she was more, I dunno, *different*. She was very nice at times. Turns out she is veeeeeery different."

"She now says her grandfather *did not* kill her husband," I said.

"Yeah? Oh, that reminds me. . . the old man you saw at the scene, the newspaper carrier you wanted me to track down? A few minutes after the shooting he saw a yellow Cadillac stop and the driver – he's pretty sure it was black man – toss something off the bridge into the Flint River. That was where they found the shotgun. New info: Yellow Cadillac, black driver."

"Not completely new. Will Black told me about the old guy seeing the yellow sedan. Sounds like the same yellow car I saw coming out of the Rollings drive."

"But Will Black has never said anything about the *driver*."

"True. Would you consider Big Cat a black man?"

"Not really," she said. "I've heard he's like mulatto or something like that. But he's so damn big, that would be remarkable enough to remember, don't you think?"

"Probably wasn't Big Cat. So he wouldn't be the one who shot Rollings."

"I'll bet he would if Lacobee told him to," Scotts said.

I nodded.

My thoughts kept drifting back to the idea that Will Black was protecting us. Maybe even trying to steer us in the right direction.

"Here's my question?" I said. "Where is Will Black in all this? At times he seems to be lending us a hand. And I'm almost certain he's connected to Manship somehow."

"What if he is? What would that mean for us?" she said.

"It would mean. . . he might give us more if we asked."

"That's what I was thinking," she said.

"That's what you were thinking?"

"Now you're repeating me. And, yes it was as a matter of fact. See?" She spun her notes around so I could read them. She tapped on a spot with her pencil. "Read right there."

There was the name she'd written in bold black letters: Will Black. It was circled.

"Okay, that's what you were thinking," I said. "So, if you had the lead now, what would you do next?"

"I'd go talk to Will Black, that's what I'd do. He knows who owns the shotgun and probably a lot more by now."

"That's what you'd do?"

"That's what I'd do *next*."

I stared at her a moment then cut my eyes away. She squirmed as she waited for my response.

"Okay," I said, looking back to her. "So then, would you go alone or take your partner?"

"Seriously? Is that a serious question?"

"It is."

She tapped her pencil and considered it. "Honestly, I would go see him alone. But wait, now…in this case only. Because I know him and he knows my dad and he obviously doesn't like you. Maybe he'd give us more if I went alone."

"He doesn't like me?"

"Ah. . . no."

"How can you tell?"

She rolled her eyes and shook her head. She began closing her notebook, picking up her notes and stuffing them into her tote.

"He really doesn't?"

She closed her eyes sadly, in mock pity, and shook her head. "Alas, no, he doesn't."

"Okay then," I said, crossing my arms. "You go. Solo."

She smiled, mouthed a confident thank you and stood. She flung the tote over her shoulder. "Now, let's go see if we can lose those two clowns in the parking lot. Sound like fun?"

"Yes, it does," I said. We raced to the door.

38

Scotts called the next day to report she'd had her one-on-one with Chief Deputy Black. It had gone well.

"You and the Chief do have that special connection," I said.

"I have my ways."

Will Black told her the shotgun they found in the river was registered to James Shyne. I recognized the name. Jimmy Shyne was a newly-elected Atlanta City Commissioner. He was an up-and-coming young black politician whose family owned a pile of real estate and commercial property, including several big-name nightclubs in the Fourth Ward. That was all I knew about him but I knew someone who'd know more.

"Will Black says the Atlanta cops are helping," she added. "And the DA's office. They're interviewing Jimmy Shyne. Will Black will fill me in on what they get. And how about this – did you know that Will Black wants to run for Sheriff next year? Our current Sheriff, Tom Fowler, and the DA don't exactly get along. And Sheriff Fowler is always out of town, like right now. He's never around."

"Cops and DAs aren't always on the best of terms. The blame game, you know."

"People around here don't like Fowler any more. They like Will Black."

"Wait until he's the one arresting them."

"He can win if he runs. Oh, and I was right, by the way. He doesn't like you. He thinks you're a smart ass."

"Where's he get that?"

"Yeah, that's a real mystery. If it's any consolation, he doesn't like *any* reporters. Except me."

"As I said, special connection."

"Maybe we do. And you ought to be glad of it."

"I am, I am. That's good work."

"Thank you."

"It's time you met someone," I said. "I'm going to set us up a meeting with Calvin Daniels. He's my former boss and was a hell of an editor years back. He knows everything there is to know about inside Atlanta. We'll meet at Drigger's. I'll let you know when."

"Cool. And I promise to be on time this time."

"That's good because once he's off the clock, he won't be sober long."

"Yeah?"

"Afraid so. Good man, though."

"Tell me when, I'll be there. I gotta go now," she said in a hasty tone.

"Dinner to cook?"

"Ha! That's rich. Travis does all the cooking. I'm going to ride for a couple of hours before he gets home. I'm getting pretty good."

"If you're going to do that, fine, just remember the fundamental: You always go where you look. You *always* go where you look."

"Okay! You've told me that already. I got it. I already have one husband, thank you." She hung up crisply.

It is true that on a motorcycle you always go where you look. Much like in investigations.

I was beginning to wonder if we were looking in the right direction.

39

CALVIN met us at Drigger's two days later – a Saturday morning after he'd worked an all-nighter at the paper. He had the jump on us, he'd already downed two longnecks by the time we arrived.

I introduced Scotts and stepped over to the bar to get him two more beers. I grabbed a coffee for Scotts and myself – what Drigger called jailhouse coffee because it sat in the pot for life. We settled in at a corner table.

"What you need to know about Jimmy Shyne is, as we say over in AA, 'if his lips are moving, he's lying,'" Calvin said. He knew his way around AA. He'd tried it several times but just couldn't buy in completely. That part about stopping drinking always hung him up.

He took a big swig and smiled at Scotts.

"They say that about politicians, too," I said.

"Yes, they do." He tipped his bottle to me and finished off the beer.

"Tell us about Jimmy Shyne. Deep background."

"You want the good stuff?" he said.

"Of course."

He grinned. "That's the part I'll miss when Manship finally has enough of my sorry ass to can me – knowing all the shit nobody else knows."

"We're wondering if our newest city commissioner is involved in our story, the Rollings killing."

"And I'm still wondering why Manship has us sitting on that one?" he said. "Any clue?"

"Nope."

"Interesting him doing that, though – you have to admit. Interesting. Anyhow, yeah, Shyne could be involved. Wouldn't surprise me. There's a lot going on down there, you know what I mean?"

"Tell us."

"I mean drugs, bookmaking, women, protection, voting fraud, hot cars – the works. It'd make sense there's a little murder and mayhem thrown in. Jimmy Shyne's old man and uncles run the dark side of town. And though the old man wants his boy legit – or at least to appear legit – I doubt you'd be out on a limb to think Jimmy-Boy has his spoon in the stew."

"How does he engage in all that, avoid the law, and still get elected to public office?" Scotts asked.

"Must be easy, everybody's doing it," Calvin said. He laughed, toasted his own joke and drank.

Scotts leaned further in and fixed her eyes on Calvin. I sat back and gave her the floor.

"Could he arrange a murder-for-hire?" she asked.

Calvin admired the question then nodded. "I'll bet he could. Easy. Lots of boys down there needing lots of money for all sorts of things. There'd be plenty of takers." He opened another beer and started in on it. "So, you two really see Shyne in something like this? How does he connect?"

"We're not sure, but the cops are looking at him," I said.

"Besides being a commissioner, what does he do?" Scotts asked. "That's a part-time job, isn't it?" she asked.

"His day job – or I should say night job – is running his old man's club down in the Fourth Ward. *Erebus,* I think the name is – some exotic name like that. As I say, all kinds of business and commerce down there. They get big name acts in their clubs, so somebody's turning some cash."

"Anything else about Mr. Shyne?" Scotts asked.

"He collects cars—I remember that from his campaign. Every TV spot showed him driving a different car. He apparently thought his constituency went for hot cars. And for all we know, the cars were hot – they have a chop shop down there somewhere, I hear."

"That's useful," Scotts said.

"And he's got quirky taste."

"Quirky taste. . . in women?" she said.

"In everything. In the shes. In the hes. And in the she-hes. He takes all comers, what I hear." He cocked his head sideways and looked at me. "Damn, Coates, I thought this was your beat. How do you not know any of this?"

"The political guys covered him while he was running. I haven't had time to catch up."

"Plus you're a slow learner," he said and again toasted his own joke.

"I'm wondering," Scotts said, again leaning in to Calvin, "if, as you say, both Shyne and Rollings had quirky tastes, would they have run into each other? Could Rollings have been a patron of Shyne's club?"

"That's possible. It's a predominantly black club, but they have private sections for wealthy patrons. Enough money involved, there are no color lines. I expect Mr. Rollings would be welcome anytime."

"How could we find out?" she asked Calvin.

"What I'd do is go ask Mr. Shyne. But be sure to…what was the question? Oh, yeah… be sure to talk to Jimmy Shyne the Commissioner, not Jimmy Shyne the gangster. Them thugs shy away from press coverage, you know. While a politician's never met a press badge he didn't like. Bet you knew that, though, didn't you, Miss …Miss—"

"That's a good point," I said. I shot Scotts a let's-wrap-this-up look. Calvin was getting close to sauced. "I'm going to settle up with Drigger, Calvin, then we'd better pull out. You look tired, man. You have a long night?"

"Did you say have a longneck? I sure will." He blinked his eyes wearily and took another long guzzle.

I walked over to the bar and asked Drigger to call Calvin a cab.

Drigger shook his head. "No need. He knows the routine. I got a cot in the storage room, I make my tossers sleep it off there. Get his keys and give them to me. He won't go anywhere."

"Done," I said. And in a couple of minutes it was. Calvin turned his keys over without resistance – like he'd been down this road a thousand times. As Scotts and I were headed out, we watched Drigger escort him to the back room. His legs were wobbly, his head slumped forward. We heard a thud as he fell into the cot. Drigger stepped out from the back a second later and gave us the thumbs up.

"That's tough," Scotts said in a shaky voice.

40

My recap notes from our first interview with Commissioner Jimmy Shyne went like this:

4/19/88, 10 a.m.

Office of City Commissioner Jimmy Shyne.

City Hall. Atlanta.

Interview re First Hundred Days in Office: tape #1988-57, to be transcribed.

Interview re Bobby Rollings: no tape.

Shyne acknowledges knowing of murder of Bobby R. Interviewed two days ago by Atlanta cops.

Says Bobby R. was one of his family's bankers, handled family Trust business.

"I didn't know Rollings well. We talked a little. We were both just two boys getting started in Old World Atlanta. Boys in an old man's game."

Shyne knows of Jacob Lacobee. Not personally. Knows of him thru Lacobee's plantation foreman, Big Cat.

Big Cat frequented Shyne's club, Erebus.

"Big Cat looks like a lion or tiger, one of those. Color of a lion, that tawny color. He's not black like the rest of us. And he always has plenty of cash. It's hard to forget a man like that."

Shyne was not aware Rollings was connected to Lacobee or Big Cat "before the killing."

Shyne was asked by cops about a yellow Cadillac he owns. Says he owns *one* now. Is a car collector and had two yellow Caddys at one time. Sold one several months ago.

Shyne says cops asked about a shotgun registered in his name. Told them he did not own any guns, knew nothing about the shotgun. Said his grandfather, also a James Shyne, was the one with the gun collection. Grandfather left collection to his father. Shyne told cops to ask his father about the shotgun.

OBSERVATION: Shyne is well-spoken, polished. Medium build, smooth handsome face, small neat mustache, short cropped Afro. Snappy dresser – wore houndstooth suit, white shirt, dark tie. Office is meticulous, organized. Secretary is June Conway, direct line 555-1047.

I had set up the appointment with Jimmy Shyne by indicating we would be doing a "First 100 Days in Office" story. I also indicated I would be bringing a partner and that we would have a few questions about the Bobby Rollings murder. He agreed to meet without conditions of any kind.

He was open and forthcoming throughout the interview. He smiled easily and never showed a moment's hesitation to answer any question. He asked about Mr. Manship as if the two of them were old chums. And he was broadly flirtatious with Scotts – that kind of flattering flirtation that was supposed to seem innocent but usually wasn't.

As we stood to leave, he stopped us with an upraised hand and asked us to stay a minute more. He stepped over and closed his office door then returned to his desk.

"Off the record?" he asked.

Scotts and I agreed.

"I'm curious," he said. "Why is the *Democrat* covering the Rollings story," – he pointed to us – "but not *reporting* anything? We don't see a word in your paper, but it's all over *The Constitution*, television, all your competitors. It's obvious, man! I mean, it looks deliberate. What's shakin'?"

"We can't say for sure, Mr. Shyne," I said. "We're just reporters, but I'd guess our editors are waiting on the full story."

"Is that usual?"

"Not really, no, but it happens. When they think the water runs deep."

"Like Watergate?"

"Maybe not on that scale."

"But *The Democrat* thinks there's more to this than just the Rollings killing?"

"That's what everybody's asking."

"Everybody?"

"The cops up here. The cops down there. State cops. Maybe even the big boys, the Feds."

"Do you know anything about that?"

"If I did, I wouldn't be able to discuss it."

"Sure, man, sure. I read you. Just curious. I'm still new to this *public servant* business. Learning I need to start paying better attention in the world, you know?"

"You need to know what's going on," Scotts threw in with a hint of sarcasm.

"Yeah, sweetlips, that's right. I need to know what's going on." He clicked a wink at her.

She clicked back. He gave her a little headshake and a body shiver, like she'd lit his fire.

"Easy now, Mr. Shyne," she said, enjoying the banter. She batted her eyes, coy. "I hardly know you."

"Hopefully we won't be strangers forever," he said with a big smile and gentleman's nod.

"I'm sure we'll be back," she said.

We exited his office with cordial handshakes. I got the distinct impression he would have liked us to stay longer. One, to see how far he could push for information on the Rollings investigations. And two, to see how far he could get with Scotts.

As we stood at the desk of his secretary, thanking her for her hospitality and getting her direct phone number, Lacey Moore strode in.

She froze as she saw me. "Coates? What are you doing here?"

"Was I supposed to be somewhere else? Like New Orleans?"

"No, no, no. I left the convention early." She seemed jittery. "It was boring and tedious. And nothing new. I'm sorry, I got in late last night. I intended to call today."

"I see," I said. "I'm glad you're back."

While I was glad to see her, she did not seem glad to see me. Her eyes darted around the room, almost shifty, as if looking for an exit. In a moment she fixed her gaze on Scotts and held it.

I broke the tableau the three of us seemed stuck in.

"Lacey, this is my new partner, Emily Scott," I said. "Emily, this is my friend, Lacey Moore. She's with the DA's office."

I was amazed how awkward this was. It shouldn't have been. It must have been the surprise of seeing her back two days early. Perhaps I was struck with the feeling that she'd snuck back into town purposefully, to avoid me. Moreover, I was asking myself, why the hell she was coming to see Jimmy Shyne? True there were plenty of criminals in City Hall, but this wasn't her normal purview.

"Pleased to meet you," Lacey said, extending her hand to Scotts as she gathered her composure. She could be cool under pressure, and frankly I liked that about her. "Coates has said you do excellent work."

"Well, thanks," Scotts said. "I followed two of your trials – the Lovell trial and the Kevin Martin case. You nailed them."

Lacey nodded, impressed, "Thank you. And, I'm sorry to have to break this off, but I have an appointment with Mr. Shyne, then I have to hurry back to meet a judge. I will talk to you tonight, Gil?"

"Oh, will you be in town?"

She arched an angry eyebrow at me then shouldered past us straight into Jimmy Shyne's office, closing the door smartly behind her.

Scotts and I headed out of the building. She said nothing. When she fell quiet like that, I could hear the storm of questions gathering in her head.

41

WE took the elevator down to the City Hall parking garage. Scotts remained silent until we got to her car.

"That was interesting," she said.

"Yes it was."

She cut her eyes my way. "I was referring to the sparring between you and Miss Moore."

"That, too."

"Something on your mind?" she asked.

"Lacey's my. . . what do they call it these days? Love interest?"

"Really? Who would have guessed? Why was she so freaked seeing you at Shyne's office?"

"You noticed?"

"It wasn't subtle."

"I don't know. Something's up. I'll figure it out. So, what did you make of Shyne?"

"Like Daniels said, every word out of his mouth is a lie."

"And the Big Cat connection?"

"He's involved, he has to be. Don't you think? I can get more on him."

"See what you can find. Be careful, he's strange."

"I like strange," she said and jumped into her Jeep. She looked around the garage. "I'll talk to Will Black, some others, see what they know about him. I'll call you. Hey, were you followed over here?"

"I don't think so," I said. "You?"

"All the way from home. That's him over there, the green car."

I glanced over. "Yep. Not one of our regulars, though. See if you can shake him. It'll be good practice. . . *Sweetlips.*"

She rolled her eyes, popped the Jeep into gear and tore out of the garage. Her tail, caught off guard, revved up his engine and squealed after her.

I walked around the garage looking for my car. I found it sitting just down from Lacey's. I decided to sit in my car and wait for her, see if we could clear things up.

While I was waiting, I spotted a tail I'd missed. There was a dark sedan parked in the far corner of the garage. It had a good sightline to my car. The shadowy driver was reading a newspaper but not very convincingly – he never turned the page.

Thirty minutes later Lacey stepped off the elevator and moved straight toward her car. She was an imposing woman, no doubt about it. Tall and lean with long confident strides; short cropped hair; dressed for power in her navy blue suit, a tan leather satchel strung over one shoulder. This day she had an especially intense look in her eyes.

She saw me as she approached and slowed as she got to my car. She took a sharp turn to my passenger door, snapped it open and climbed in. She slammed the door and without warning lit in.

"You and I are done," she said. "You understand? Done. The end. Finished."

"What the hell are you talking about?"

"I'm calling this off, right now."

"What? Why? I don't get it? Because I questioned your honesty?"

She stared, furious at the suggestion. "I have not. . .I haven't lied to you." She turned away. "This doesn't work for me any more, that's all."

"I know the deal, Lacey. Nobody else from your office went to a goddamn convention. No one."

"I never said they did."

"It makes me wonder. Did you go to a convention? And if not, why would you lie about it?"

She held her eyes forward a long while then turned to me. "I go *where,* and I do *what* my boss tells me. That's my job."

"I know that."

"I do what I need to do. And right now that means shutting this down. You and I are done. Don't resist, please. Don't say anything more." She threw open the door and stepped out. She turned and leaned in. "I'm sorry. I really am. But I. . .I'm sorry."

"I am too."

"I promised I'd tell you if you were ever stepping in deep shit. Well, now you are." She slammed the door.

As she moved toward her car, the dark sedan I'd spotted earlier came spinning around the corner, headed toward her. For a moment she didn't see the car or the speed it was gathering. As it got closer, it swerved right at her. She looked up in time to see it and jump between two parked cars. The sedan clipped the back ends of the cars, caromed across the way, sideswiped a concrete pillar then sped toward the exit.

I was out of my car and over to her in a second. In the time it took me to get there, she'd already pulled her gun and pointed it at the tail of the fleeing sedan. She glanced over, saw me coming and lowered the gun.

"Fucker's out of range anyway," she muttered.

"Jesus, Lacey, are you okay?"

She looked at me a second without a pinch of fear in her eyes. "Yeah, I'm okay."

"What the hell was that?"

She shoved the gun back in her satchel.

"Looked like a goddamn drunk driver to me," she said without looking my way.

"You're crazy! That guy came right at you! Deliberately. I saw him do it."

She tried to dismiss the idea but didn't convince me.

"I saw his eyes, Lacey, he was looking right at you."

"You're wrong. It was a drunk. I have to go inside and call this in. You need to get out of here. You shouldn't have been here, anyway. As far as I'm concerned, you weren't. Leave, Coates."

She turned and walked briskly toward the elevator. Without looking back she called out again, "Leave, Coates. Leave."

42

THE hit-and-run scare had been for Lacey, not me. I was sure of that. If I'd been the target, the driver would have had plenty of cracks at me earlier while I was roaming the garage looking for my car.

This had been a warning shot. The driver hadn't aimed to kill her, or even hit her – that much was obvious. He'd made too much noise. His swerves had been calculated. I was certain he'd slowed a little to give her time to get out of the way.

So if this was some kind of warning to Lacey, or to the DA's office, what were they looking at? Targeting a District Attorney – even with a phony baloney effort like that – was an extreme measure. They must be onto something that mattered a lot to someone.

But did it matter to us?

I tried imagining what Lacey could be working on and how it might connect to our story. She rarely worked anything but white collar crimes; ours was a small-town murder. As far as we knew, Jimmy Shyne's only connection to the Rollings killing was the shotgun – and that actually belonged to his grandfather, not him. But was there more? Was Shyne, Rollings and the DOJ investigation all one big ball of twine we just hadn't unwound yet?

The abrupt breakup had cast the shadow of suspicion. Not that I hadn't imagined the possibility of Lacey walking on me. But this had been far too spontaneous for her. She deliberated everything at length – it took her an hour-and-a-half to order breakfast at a short-order grill. She never shot from the hip – she wasn't a *ready-fire-aim* kind of woman. And yet, she had done just that, just now. Right after a chance encounter in Jimmie Shyne's office.

Very uncharacteristic. *Suspiciously* uncharacteristic.

Last but not least was the matter of the lie – the New Orleans convention she never attended. I had discovered it inadvertently when I'd run into another ADA downtown and had asked how he had avoided convention duty. He had no idea what I was talking about. He knew of no one from his office at a convention.

My conclusion was she'd gone somewhere, just not to a convention. It wouldn't have been a rendezvous, either. If Lacey ever wanted another lover, she would simply take one, open and above board. Of that I was sure.

So where, then? Where had she been? What was she after?

I spent the next few days digging into those questions.

I made all my rounds and got nothing. I called Gary Hooper in Washington. He couldn't help. I made a second pass at all my contacts and got a lot more of the same: Nothing. For three days I knocked on doors and got nowhere.

On the fourth day, a door finally opened. Fireman First Class Denny Thames had what I was looking for.

"Fire for profit," he said.

Thames had been the chief arson investigator for the Metro Fire Department for almost thirty years. He had spent a good part of that time sifting through cinders down in the Fourth Ward.

"They buy these old buildings cheap, insure them for plenty, do some half-ass remodeling, then burn 'em down. Big bucks in it."

"Who does that?" I asked.

"Who do you think?" he said. "It'd be a name you'd recognize, I can tell you that."

"Is the District Attorney working with you?"

"I finally got their attention. By my figures, these bastards have made over ten million bucks in the last five years. Numbers like that, the DA can't ignore. So they assigned a couple lawyers and an investigator."

"Lacey Moore one of those?"

"Yeah, fetching young gal. She's tough, too. You know her?"

"I do. Covered a couple of her trials."

"She and some kid just out of law school are working it. Guess she's training him. And they got that investigator, what's his name, very sharp guy."

"Jay Plummer?"

"Yeah, that's him. Jay's been doing most of the leg work for them. I give him everything I get on it. He's good."

"Where are they?"

"I think they're closing in on the bastards. Good riddance, too. They've burned down half the ward. Making Sherman's march look like child's play."

"Would I be right in guessing the Shyne family are the 'bastards' you refer to?"

Thames nodded. "That'd be a good guess."

I knew Jay Plummer well enough to invite him to Drigger's for a beer. He knew me well enough to accept. We met early evening and took a seat at the bar. Drigger served us each a longneck.

Jay was a stocky, curly-haired fellow who had been a DA investigator for years. He was a tough-minded, by-the-book guy. Lacey says no one can pull the pieces together better.

"If you're thinking I'm going to be your Deep Throat, Coates, you're wrong," Plummer said. He tipped his bottle to mine. I assured him I wasn't looking for one.

"Good," he said. "And I'm not going to be the go-between for you and Lacey."

"I wouldn't ask you to."

"Good. So what do you want?"

"A few answers to a few questions."

"Go ahead. We'll see."

"Just don't forget how much we helped you guys on that Hardaman case," I reminded him.

He nodded, grinned and took a sip.

I told him what I'd learned from Denny Thames about the arson-for-profit ring. Then I recounted the hit-and-run attempt on Lacey – my version not hers.

"Could those two things be connected?" I asked.

"I thought she said it was some drunk nearly hit her."

"Not the way I saw it. It was deliberate and it was for her. So, could that be related to the arson investigation?"

"What would you guess?"

"I'd guess it is."

"That might be a good guess."

"Second question. Could there be a connection between the fires and the murder of this banker back on Easter Sunday, guy named Bobby Rollings?"

He took another sip. "What did he do for a living, this Rollings fellow?"

"Investments. Georgia Commerce Bank. Oh, and he ran with some of that Fourth Ward crowd."

"Investments, you say? Interesting." Jay tapped his empty on the bar and Drigger served him another. "So, this Rollings fellow would have the money to lend somebody for the purchase of, say, buildings?"

"He wasn't a loan officer."

"He directed investments? He was an investor?"

"That's right."

"Well, I'd say if you were an investor, you would be needing places to invest your money. And if somebody bought buildings to burn for profit, they'd be needing money to buy them. Wouldn't they? That sound like a potential connection to you?"

I smiled. "It does."

"So my *guess* would be, yes, they could be connected."

I considered what he'd just told me. I sipped my beer slowly. Plummer struck up a conversation with Drigger. When they'd finished chatting and he'd polished off his second beer, he set the bottle down firmly.

"That's it for me. Two's my limit," he said. "Is that all? That all you want?"

"I did have one small personal question, but since you've already declined matchmaking duty—"

"Oh, no, buddy, I'm not getting in the middle of that. No way, Jose. I like my job too much. See you. Thanks for the beers." He started away then paused, tapped his finger on the bar. "We did say this was off the record, didn't we?"

I nodded yes.

"Okay, so is this: You could be onto something with that connection you were talking about, Rollings and Shyne."

"You sure?"

"Positive."

"That's helpful, Jay. Since I never mentioned the Shynes."

"You didn't? I'll be damned. A slip-of-the-tongue. Looks like I need to lower my limit to one."

He tapped the bar again and walked off smiling.

43

SIDEBAR:
"Fourth Ward Building Fire Kills Two"

Excerpted from: *The Atlanta Democrat*
February 9, 1988

ATLANTA, Ga. — Two men are dead in a late night fire in Atlanta's Fourth Ward that destroyed an historic old hotel and burned for over four hours, according to Atlanta Deputy Fire Chief Tanner Cherry. Metro firemen fought the blaze from 11 p.m. Tuesday until shortly after 5 a.m. Wednesday.

"The victims were burned beyond recognition, it will take some time to identify the bodies," Cherry said.

The four-story Buckhalter Hotel appears to be a total loss, Cherry said. Located at 700 South Boulevard, The Buckhalter was most recently a low-cost transient hotel. It was permanently closed some two years ago, though authorities believe transients still often used the abandoned building for shelter in extreme weather.

While the fire is the suspected cause of death for both victims, it has not been officially determined, Cherry said. Investigators say initial findings suggest arson.

This fire marks the third major building fire in the Fourth Ward in the past year, but this is the first with fatalities, Cherry said. Arson is also suspected in the first two fires.

The Buckhalter is owned by Gray Poppa Enterprises, a property management company headed by brothers Jerome and Gerald Shyne. Restoration of the property had gotten underway some six months earlier and was nearing completion, according to a spokesman for the company.

Already in Georgia this year the State Fire Marshal has investigated 47 fires, 22 of which were deemed arsons. Suspects have been arrested in three of the cases, according to James Huckabay, executive director of the Georgia Insurance Information Service.

Authorities don't know a motive for this latest Fourth Ward fire, but unknown motive is no surprise in an arson, they say.

"Arson has a remarkably low conviction rate," said Webb Smith, president of the Georgia Underwriting Association, which sponsors Georgia Arson Control. The group offers a reward for information that convicts an arsonist.

"Only 4 to 6 percent of people ever charged with arson are convicted," Smith said. "There are many motives for arson, including fires to conceal crimes, revenge and insurance fraud."

Georgia Arson Control provides a toll-free tip line (1-800-555-8280) for information, with rewards of up to $10,000. In the first three months of this year, the Arson Hotline has received 11 calls regarding arson cases.

The following is the latest data provided by the U.S. Fire Protection Association:

–In 1987, arsonists set fires that destroyed $332 million in property in the U.S.

–In 1987, there were 14,400 intentionally set structure fires in the U.S.

–In 1987, the number of deaths in arson fires totaled 112 in the U.S.

44

Scotts called later that day to tell me she had gotten very little on Big Cat and that Will Black had been dodging her for three days. When she finally caught him at his office he wouldn't talk to her. He said he wanted to see both of us there tomorrow at one o'clock. She told him we'd be there.

She asked me to ride my bike down early and meet her at a road-side park north of town. She wanted to show me something.

The next day was bright and sunny, perfect for a bike ride. I rolled up to the park a little before 11 a.m. Scotts was already there, sitting happily astride a new motorcycle. It was a shiny black BMW 650. She looked downright jaunty in her tight riding jacket, knee length boots and long blonde hair flowing from her helmet. More like an English lady decked out for a fox hunt.

While I didn't know my BMWs that well, this looked like a recent model, no more than a couple of years old. From the hum of the engine, it sounded in good shape.

She didn't wait for me to come to a stop. She pulled down her visor and signaled to follow. She took off, I fell in behind her.

We crisscrossed the north end of the Latham County, cruising the back roads and leaning low into all the twisties we could find. She handled the bike with the confidence of a veteran, though she did take one turn too hot and ended up bounding out into a grassy field. She managed to keep the bike upright, though, and get back on the road without dumping it.

After an hour, she slowed. We were on FM 71, a narrow blacktop that ran through a festooned stretch of hardwoods and small pines. This looked a lot like the wooded area north of the Rollings home.

She eased over to a shoulder and came to a stop in the shade. We killed the engines, doffed the helmets and soaked in the soft humming of the woods. It was quiet out there. We hadn't seen any traffic in at least a half hour.

Scotts reached into her tank bag, pulled out binoculars and stepped over to the tree line. She pointed through the thick trees and raised the glasses. "See down there?" she said in a hush. "That's the Rollings place."

She handed me the binoculars. I strained to make out the roofline, then the sharp angular architecture of the house. "Barely, but I see it. Yeah, that's it."

"You can see better at night when they have the lights on down there."

"How do you know that?"

"How do you *think* I know that?"

"I can guess."

"It's perfect. I can see them, they can't see me!"

I didn't want to encourage the idea. I moved to the more immediate one. "What time did you say we're meeting Will Black?"

She looked at her watch. "Oh shit, one o'clock. We need to hightail it."

Will Black was standing outside the side entrance smoking a cigarette as we pulled into the parking lot. He watched with amusement as we stood the bikes in a far corner and hurried his way.

He flicked his cigarette and waved us into the building then back to his office. We sat and accepted the coffee he offered.

"So what have we got here, The Wild Bunch?" he said with a minor smirk.

"My new transportation. I'm still learning," Scotts told him. She looked over to me, "Hey, what do you think of the new bike? Cool, huh?" She turned quickly back to Will Black. "He's teaching me to ride safely."

"Not sure he knows how to do anything safely," Black muttered as he stuck his big paw into his desk drawer and pulled out a file folder. He glanced over it a second then closed it and looked at us. He began rocking back and forth in his desk chair. "So you two want to know about Big Cat, that right?"

"We have several questions, but that'll do for starters," I said. "Can we take notes?"

He shook his head. We put our pads away.

"What I got to tell you is ears only," he said. "It's only about half true, anyway. Trouble is, I don't know which half."

"We'll take whatever you've got," Scotts said.

"Scary fella, this one," he said. "Big Cat is a Mulatto, not a Negro like all the whites around here think. And for some reason, the Mulattos scare the Negros. Don't know why that is, but it's true. The story goes that Lacobee bought him off a Louisiana cotton farmer thirty years ago, when Cat was a kid. I wouldn't doubt that part, by the way. Lacobee raised him like a son. He counts on him for everything."

"Everything would include?" Scotts asked.

"Everything," Black said. "Some might suspect that if Lacobee wanted Bobby Rollings dead – which I figure he did – he'd have Big Cat do it. I don't think so. I don't think he'd put Cat in that position."

"Why's that?"

"Call it gut. And as you see, I got a substantial one, so I trust it substantially."

Scotts laughed out loud. Will Black gave her a look and a nod.

"Where'd he get the name?" Scotts asked.

"Don't know. Maybe the girl gave it to him back when she was a kid. His given name is Leon Metoyer."

"Lorelei named him Big Cat?"

"Could be. They're about the same age, more or less grew up together, as I understand it." Black stopped a moment as if taking on a new thought, then went on. "Anyhow, the hands out there on the plantation think he's a beast. Every one of 'em scared shitless of him. Heard 'em say he could kill a man with his bare hands. Heard others say he has."

"Has he?" I asked.

Will Black shrugged.

"What does your gut say?" Scotts asked.

"Maybe. No evidence of it, though."

"How come?"

"Nobody knows or sees anything out there. Lacobee and his place are all off limits. Per Sheriff Fowler and the DA. They make the final calls, and I s'pose they haven't seen any calls to make. So, if Lacobee did have anything to do with killing Rollings, he gets a free pass."

"That doesn't sit well with you. We get it. But why are you telling us?" I said. "Sounds like a local problem."

"That it is. You're right."

Scotts gave me an annoyed glare then turned back to Black.

"So your hands are tied, Chief?" she asked.

"More or less. Mine are, but yours ain't."

Scotts and I glanced at one another. I gave her a go-ahead nod.

"What are you suggesting?" she said cautiously. "Where would you start if you had free rein?"

"I'd start with the boy. He saw the shooter. Now you two wouldn't know that, but I do. The Sheriff and the DA would never in a million years let me question him. But you," and he looked right at Scotts, "you might be able to talk to him. In a roundabout way. Don't you know Lorelei?"

"I do."

"There you go. A couple of photos of suspects to show the boy and you got a starting place."

"Suspects like. . ."

"Like Jimmy Shyne, for one. And Big Cat for another."

"I thought your gut ruled Cat out," she said.

"My gut's been wrong before," he said, tilting back and patting his belly tenderly, as if consoling it for the insult.

We all three sat quietly for a moment. Will Black rocked in his chair steadily and watched us.

"Sounds risky," I said. "Not two days ago you were trying to scare us off, telling us how goddamn dangerous it was around here."

"I can do this," Scotts murmured to me. I ignored her.

"The Rollings woman is not the most stable person in the world," I went on. "What are you trying to get us into?"

"Stay calm, son. I'm not trying to get you into anything you don't want into." He scratched his chin, rubbed the side of his fleshy face. "Just a thought. Something for you to think about. But, if you can't do it—"

"I can do it, dammit," Scotts said loudly to both us. "I *want* to do it."

"I know you do, but that woman, I've seen her in action," I said. "If she catches you trying to—"

"Will this help you a lot, Chief?" she asked.

"Sure it'll help me. Help you, too, though." He turned a questioning look to me.

"We'll discuss it," I said.

"You do that and let me know. Meanwhile, I gotta get back to work. And you two need to run along."

He rose quickly and escorted us to the outer door. He opened it onto the lot and shook his head, again amused by our motorcycles.

"By the way," he said, grinning, "my boys tell me you're onto them."

"Yes, you're following us," Scotts snapped. "And I don't like that!"

"Serve and protect, sugar, *serve and protect* – just like it says on our cars." He grinned bigger then closed the door on us.

We walked slowly to our bikes, digesting what Will Black had told us: Jimmy Shyne was a key suspect; the cops needed to know who and what the kid saw; and he didn't intend to stop having us followed – or, as he put it, "protected."

"I don't need any damn protection," Scotts muttered out of the side of her mouth as she got on her bike and waited for me to mount mine. "I can handle this, you know. And if the boy *did* see who shot his father, we need to find out – "

"I know you can handle it. Calm down. I wanted to see how far he'd go."

"Damn, Coates! You were playing him? Really? I wish you'd let me in on it when you're going to pull something like that!"

"It was spontaneous."

"Yeah, right. So tell me why I'm beginning to think there's more to this than just who killed Bobby Rollings?"

"Because there is."

"What? What else?"

"We won't know that until the boss tells us."

She wrinkled her brow and slipped on her sunglasses.

We heard a loud thump and looked over at a patrol car that had taken the turn into the parking lot too sharp and had caught some curb. The driver pulled up close to the side entrance and stepped out hurriedly.

It was Scotts' cousin, Boyd O'Con. She drew his attention with a big wave and smile. He was unsure for a moment who the blonde on the motorcycle was. When he finally recognized her, he gave her a small, reluctant nod and hustled inside.

"He and Weaver, they're both getting weird," she said, snapping down her visor. "Or *more* weird, I should say. Anyhow, follow me, I have one more thing to show you."

Fifteen minutes later we were back on FM 71 overlooking the Rollings house. We rolled past it, through the hills and into a flat, wooded landscape. We came out of a turn, out of the woods and into a long straightaway with cultivated fields on both sides. She pulled over to the shoulder and left her bike running. I eased up beside her.

"Right over there," she pointed across the field, "that's where we were the other day. Just the other side of that tree line is the pond where Lacobee and Big Cat were killing the hogs."

"Okay. I see that."

"Good. Follow me."

As we continued down the road, it narrowed to a one-lane mix of asphalt and gravel – not the best surface for a motorcyclist, especially a newcomer. I watched her carefully. She was handling it well enough to stay upright. Another mile and she came to a stop. Off to the right was a trailhead, then a narrow, rocky trail that crossed a culvert and ran off deep into the woods.

"I don't think we're getting in there on these," I said to her.

"Well, no," she said. "But if you ever wanted to go to DeRussey, this is the back door."

"The cemetery?"

"That's where they buried Bobby Rollings. It's nearly a mile back up in there. This takes you right to it."

"And we know this because. . ."

"Because I walked in yesterday. Found his grave. And about a million old ones – it's creepy, I'll tell you."

"Damn, Scotts."

"Don't get all panicky. I knew where everybody was. They were clearing a field way on the other side of the plantation. Lacobee, Cat, the whole crew was over there. What do you think, I'm crazy?"

"No comment."

"Anyhow, if you ever want to see where Bobby Rollings is buried, that's where it is."

"Great."

"You don't sound enthused. But let me tell you, you never know. Remember that. You. Never. Know."

"Got it. You never know. Can we roll now?"

"Sure. Think you can find your way home from here?" she said.

I nodded and pulled my helmet on.

"Where'd you get the new bike?" I asked.

"Travis got it for me up in Atlanta."

"Nice ride. Lucky you."

She danced her eyebrows. "Lucky Travis!"

I laughed and revved my engine.

"C'mon. Race you back to the highway."

45

Two days later, Scotts visited Lorelei Rollings at the plantation. She took a file photo we'd found of Jimmy Shyne, a mug shot of Big Cat that Will Black provided, and a photo of a man named Ardis Cash that Black also gave her. He didn't bother to explain why he'd included Ardis Cash. He said he'd elaborate if she got any response from the boy.

The visit began well enough. She'd seen Jacob Lacobee in the field on his tractor as she'd come onto the grounds. He'd even touched his hat to her as she passed. She'd been cheerily welcomed inside by Eva Lacobee. And Lorelei not only remembered her, she welcomed her with a warm embrace and invited her to her suite in the upstairs south wing.

When they entered the suite, the boy, Scotts said, was sitting quietly on the floor of the parlor room playing with small toys. She and Lorelei, still in her morning robe, sat in the parlor for a time, had a cup of coffee and reminisced about high school. Scotts was up front about working for the *Atlanta Democrat* and told Lorelei she hoped to be able to interview her one day for a human interest story – a story on the difficulties of raising a young boy as a single mother. Lorelei was agreeable to the idea, Scotts said.

After a lengthy chat, Lorelei excused herself to her bedroom and Scotts had a chance to show the photos to the boy. He was unresponsive. She went through the photos a second time. Still not a word, just that blank stare and frozen silence. She quickly put the photos away and returned to her coffee.

The boy had remained trance-like but was startled out of it when his mother re-entered the room. When he saw her, he yelped, turned away and skittered to a far corner.

Lorelei was furious with his behavior. She snatched him up by the arm and pulled him into the other room. Her voice was shrill, her words harsh and mean-spirited, Scotts said.

When she returned to the parlor several minutes later, she moved slowly and had a spacy gaze. Scotts guessed she was into the jimsonweed again. Or something. Lorelei moved close to Scotts, cozied up and began touching and rubbing her arms. She allowed her morning robe to loosen and fall open as she delicately touched the buttons on Scotts' blouse. In a moment she was pushing her naked breast into Scotts' open blouse and bending in to kiss her.

Scotts admitted she let Lorelei kiss her. And that she let the kiss linger, had felt a warm shiver and a thrill. A part of her wanted to let Lorelei go on, " to see what it was like." But that was the smaller part of her.

The bigger part pulled back. "I'm sorry, Lorelei, I can't do this," Scotts said.

Lorelei jerked away. "What do you want, then? You and you're goddamn newspaper. Were you talking to Robert just now?"

"Yes, I was. But only to say hello to him. He's a beautiful boy."

"Liar. That's a lie. You're after something. You're after him, aren't you? You're trying to take him away from me. You think I'm not fit."

"No, Lorelei, that's not it at all. I don't think that. Nobody does."

"I know what you think. You all think. You think I killed my husband, don't you? But I didn't. I didn't!" Her voice had gained intensity with every word, growing louder and louder. "It was him!"

She pointed downstairs. She screamed and flailed at the air. "It was him! It was him! It was my grandfather, that's who!"

Eva Lacobee and the maid must have heard the screaming and hurried upstairs. They opened the door, and Eva Lacobee rushed over to Lorelei. She wrapped her arms around her and held her tightly. She pulled her head into her chest and smoothed her hair with her hand. Lorelei began sobbing. The maid hurried into the bedroom to tend the boy.

As the room fell quiet, Scotts saw the sadness and weariness on Eva Lacobee's face. Scotts lowered her eyes and said she would see herself out. She apologized for the intrusion and for upsetting Lorelei.

Eva Lacobee nodded understanding and apologized, herself, for the sudden sad circumstances. "It will take this poor child some time to mend," she whispered to Scotts as she turned to leave the room. "Maybe you can visit her another time."

"Yes ma'am, Miss Eva. Thank you."

In the meantime, I dug up information on Ardis Cash, the new name we'd gotten from Will Black. I learned from my cop pals that he was a well-known Fourth Ward thug who could pull together any kind of outlaw operation you were interested in, from arson to murder-for-hire and anything in-between. He wasn't associated with anyone specifically, he was a freelancer. But he had often worked as a bouncer in the Shyne family clubs over the years. As far as my guys knew, he'd never worked directly for Jimmy Shyne, only his father and uncles.

To my question of whether the Atlanta cops were looking into the Rollings murder – and if so, were the Shynes connected – I got zip. Hit a stone wall. One cop did offer a hint, though it was one I'd already gotten: "Call Denny Thames over at Metro Fire," he'd said. "If anyone is looking at the Shynes, it'll be him."

I also spent time trying to get in touch with Lacey – not to learn anything about her work but to see if she was intractable on the breakup. If refusing to take my call was intractable, the answer was clear.

The day after Scotts had her lovefest with Lorelei Rollings, I got a call from Mrs. Christian. She wanted to arrange a meeting with Mr. Manship. He had expressly asked that I bring my partner, Mrs. Scott. It would be a dinner meeting, Mrs. Christian said, in a private room at Mr. Manship's Country Club. Whatever evening would be convenient for the two of us would be fine for him, though he would prefer within the next few nights if possible. I told her we would be there the next evening.

46

OUR dinner meeting with Mr. Manship was set for 8 p.m. I asked Scotts to meet me at the paper early with the promise to give her a tour of the newsroom, introduce her around, then drive us to the meeting.

She arrived as I was parking. She stepped out of her orange Jeep dressed to the nines. She wore long, slender charcoal pants, a square shouldered jacket, a white blouse with high cut collar and long draping black scarf. Her mane of blonde hair flowed down and over her shoulders. This was not the Scotts I'd been accustomed to seeing.

"I hope I'm not overdressed," she said.

"If you were intending to make me look underdressed, it worked," I said.

"That wouldn't be hard to do," she said. "Can we go inside, it's windy out here. My hair, you know."

I took her around the newsroom and introduced her to several of the weekend reporters. We stuck our heads in Calvin's office. He greeted me with a nod and Scotts with a "Wow!" I told him we were meeting the boss for dinner shortly. He extended a hand.

"Good for you," Calvin said. "And there I was thinking you'd be cleaning the presses before long."

On the drive to the club, which took thirty minutes or so, I briefed Scotts on the few meetings I'd had with Mr. Manship. I assured her he was easy to talk to.

"He's well traveled, interested in everything, and tells elaborate stories," I said. "His theme, if he had one, would be 'Be Everywhere, Know Everything.'"

"Okay, now you're really making me nervous," she said. She pulled the visor mirror down to check her makeup. "Oh shit, I forgot the blush and I don't have any. Do I look too pale?"

I glanced over but in the fading light of evening couldn't see much.

"Never mind, I got this. Slow down a sec, will you?"

I slowed. She touched her pinky to the bright red lipstick she wore and then rubbed a little color into each cheek. After a couple of dabs and vigorous rubs, she flipped the visor up.

"Okay, done. Proceed."

We reached the country club a little early. I pulled into the lane marked for Valet Parking and waited in line behind two Mercedes. The parking lot was full of big, black cars and teeming with young men in bright white slacks and vests taking keys, parking cars, darting to and from the valet stand.

Inside, a host greeted us and said that Mr. Manship would be up to meet us shortly; he wished us to enjoy a drink in the lounge meanwhile.

We moved into the lounge and took a seat at a small table. A waiter took our order. The lounge was bustling. Groups of chattering couples filled most of the tables. There was an enclave of nattily attired young men – scions no doubt of wealthy members – standing at the bar, surveying the place and offering one another jokey asides. They were what Lacey referred to as "cocks of the walk," and they seemed to be doing their best to honor that as their ideal. On the less-than-ideal side, they were getting louder and drunker by the minute.

As our drinks arrived, Scotts excused herself to the powder room. The band of young gents at the bar let their ogling eyes follow as she walked past.

Several minutes later she stepped around the corner from the ladies room and was headed back to the table when one of the fellows, the tallest of the bunch, stepped in front of her, stopped her progress. She smiled and spoke pleasantly to him. They conversed for a minute or more.

As she gave him a polite parting nod and started to step away, he moved to block her. She flashed him a cautionary look. He ignored it and stepped closer to her, as if trying to whisper in her ear. She gave him a warning look and a quiet word or two, probably about his increasingly unseemly behavior. I stood up and headed toward her, but she saw me move out of the corner of her eye and raised a finger.

Okay, she had this. Didn't surprise me. I stopped.

Apparently Mr. Cock hadn't fully understood her caution. He moved closer still, pressed his body into hers and leaned in as if aiming for a kiss. She reached down, grabbed his belt buckle and tugged him in to her. She curled her right foot behind his ankles and gently pushed him backward. He went tumbling to the floor. Laughter erupted from his band of buddies at the bar.

"Oh my god!" Scotts exclaimed. "I'm so sorry, let me help you up."

She leaned over to offer her hand but he refused. He jumped up and stared at her. He took an aggressive step toward her but she threw up her hand and stopped him. By now, the lounge had fallen quiet.

"Not your best option," she said evenly. "I have a small caliber pistol somewhere on my person and while it won't kill you, it can ruin your love life forever."

Another round of laughter rolled across the lounge. The fellow glared at her a moment then stepped aside.

I had retreated back to our table and as she approached, I felt a hand from behind on my shoulder. I turned to see Mr. Manship.

He'd been standing there watching the episode unfold. He leaned in and whispered to me with a touch of admiration, "Plucky!"

"Yes sir, she is."

I formally introduced Scotts to Mr. Manship, then he ushered us out of the lounge and through a labyrinth of long, richly carpeted hallways to a private sitting room. He pushed open the big wooden door.

"We'll dine in here," he said, and added with a smile to Scotts, "away from the common rabble."

She smiled and nodded thanks.

The room was plush and cozy. On the far wall were floor-to-ceiling mahogany shelves lined with thick books, awards and trophies, photos of famous golfers like Ben Hogan and Sam Snead. The shelves framed a stone fireplace with a small fire going. Rich red tapestry rugs sat on dark wood floors. The walls were cream colored, with white trim; warm wooden beams hatched the ceiling, concealing soft, low lighting. On the far side of the room was a wall of windows offering a look out onto the now dusky golf course.

Mr. Manship took a large rolled leather chair near the fireplace and invited us to sit in similar chairs opposite. He touched a button on some device on his side table and the draperies across the windows glided shut.

"We'll order in a minute," he said, "but I'm curious, Mrs. Scott. Do you have a small caliber pistol somewhere on your person?"

Without a blink she said, "If I told, it would ruin the element of surprise."

Mr. Manship laughed heartily. "I like your panache, young lady."

"Thank you, sir," she said demurely. "I think. Ah, this is really a beautiful place here."

"I'll pass the compliment along. As you see, the advantage of wealth – it enables one to build fancier illusions. Or maybe that's a disadvantage…I've never been sure which."

We both laughed and relaxed.

Mr. Manship asked Scotts to tell him more about herself, and she did. He then asked about her life in Latham County. She told him she'd been born and raised there and while she knew little else, couldn't imagine a better life.

"And you have ambitions to be a journalist?"

"Yes sir, I do."

"Those are fine ambitions. And Will Black? You know him I understand? I believe you both do?"

We nodded.

"Without saying anything more, I'd like to ask you to give Chief Black the benefit of the doubt. He's a friend of ours." When he said the word "ours" he circled his hand in the air to include the three of us. "You with me?"

"Yes, sir," we both responded.

"So, he's not following us, he really *is* protecting us?" Scotts blurted.

Mr. Manship nodded slightly. "As I said, allow him the benefit of the doubt."

I'd been almost certain Will Black had been the one who'd alerted Mr. Manship to the Rollings murder. Vague as he may have wanted to remain about that, he just confirmed it for me.

Mr. Manship had turned toward Scotts and was gazing at her admiringly. She noticed it and after a moment began to shift a little in her chair. He saw her unease and spoke again.

"You may not know this, Mrs. Scott – or you either for that matter, Mr. Coates – but I once lived in Latham County. That was decades ago, in my youth. We were there only a half dozen years. My father was an itinerant farm hand and later a foreman for the cotton farmers."

"Really?" she said. "Then you know all about the country life."

"I suppose I do. Some."

"And did you know Mr. Lacobee? When you were a boy? He said you did."

"Yes, I did. He was older, though. My brother's age. They were acquainted."

He had already told me, but I wanted Scotts to hear this so I asked, "That was the brother you spoke of before, sir, the one who was shot and killed?"

"Yes, it was. But," he shifted in his chair and reached for the phone on the side table, "no more tragic memories for now. Shall we order?"

We did and a short time later a waiter rolled our meals in on a fancy wood cart.

As we ate, we told Mr. Manship what we knew so far and where we thought the story was headed. When we got to Jimmy Shyne, he perked up.

"How do you think he is involved?"

"It appears the Shynes are operating an arson-for-profit scheme down in the Fourth Ward," I said. "Bobby Rollings managed several big family trusts, including the Shyne's, so he knew them. Investigators suspect he was channeling investor funds to the Shynes to buy buildings, do a cheap fix-up, then burn them down and collect the insurance. It's possible Rollings and Jimmy Shyne got crossways, Shyne did something about it."

"That wouldn't be Jimmy Shyne," Mr. Manship said with certainty. "He's not in the family business. His father wants him legitimate, and I suspect he is. I met with him before he ran for City Commissioner. He asked for our support. We didn't endorse him, but we didn't go the other way either. We told him we'd have to wait and see, give him a trial period."

"So you don't think Jimmy Shyne had anything to do with the Rollings murder?" Scotts asked.

"No. I wouldn't rule out his father, though."

"Could his father be connected to Jacob Lacobee?" Scotts asked.

"Good question, Mrs. Scott. What do you think?"

"Well, sir," she glanced uneasily at me then pressed on. "This whole thing is so weird. I mean, the idea of having someone murdered on Easter Sunday. A shotgun to the face. That's nasty, yes, but eerie, too.

"Then there was the funeral service – very creepy, even for us Baptists. And burying him in the family plot, DeRussey, which everybody says is some kind of killing field.

"And Lorelei Rollings – she's either deranged or drugged-up or both. She even shot at us – did Coates tell you that? – though she was all zoomed-up on jimsonweed at the time. So, Big Cat said.

"And Big Cat. There's one spooky creature for you.

"I mean. . . the whole thing is so *crazy*, it seems like it would take a crazy to do it. And Jacob Lacobee, who everyone thinks killed Bobby Rollings – I did too, at first – is a lot of things, but crazy isn't one of them."

"Meaning?" Manship asked.

"What if it's Lorelei?"

"There you go," Mr. Manship said and eased back in his chair. He closed his eyes and leaned his head on the rest. "A good question. Very good."

We sat silent until he opened his eyes.

Scotts added hastily, "I didn't express that very well. I'm a better writer than I am a talker, I promise. And you understand, I'm not positive about Lorelei."

"No, no. But anything possible to be imagined is an image of the truth."

"Is it?" she asked, then added, "Oh, wow, I like that! What did you say again, sir?"

"Anything possible to be imagined is an image of the truth."

"Man, oh man!" Scotts said. Her eyes were dancing with excitement.

"That's why we go wherever the story takes us, right?" he said.

"Yes, sir. Right. That's right." She sat awed and adoring now, hanging on his every word.

"Mr. Manship, we are also wondering…have you ever heard of a man named Ardis Cash?" I asked.

"No. I don't believe I have. Where does he fit in?"

I was about to tell him when an attendant in a crisp white shirt and black vest tapped on the door then stepped in and handed him a note. The attendant waited as Mr. Manship read the note.

"Tell him I'll be along in a moment," Mr. Manship said. The attendant hurried from the room.

"I am sorry to have to break this off, there's a man here I must speak to before he leaves," Manship said. "Can we resume right where we are at our next meeting?"

"Yes, sir, we can," we said and stood. We thanked him for dinner.

"My pleasure. And press on, let the story take you where it will." He rose and escorted us to the door. "I trust you can find your way out? Follow the hall to your left."

"Yes, sir, we can."

He smiled at Scotts. "And Mrs. Scott, stay out of our lounge for tonight. It appears to be filled with people whose minds are not cluttered with learning."

She gave him a large smile, a nod, and started out.

Mr. Manship pulled me aside a moment and said quietly, "I want her paid well and brought along fast. She gets it."

"Yes, sir," I said.

As we made our way down the hall I could see Scotts was anxious.

"What was that? That whisper? What did he say? Am I fired? That stuff with that guy in the bar, the gun. . .that was too much, wasn't it?"

I looked at her soberly a moment then let a smile appear. "It was less than the asshole deserved. But, no, you're good."

"Not fired?"

"Not fired. In fact, he said to bring you along fast. That sound like a dismissal?"

"Well, no. Hell no!" She looked at me wide eyed and started to erupt. She caught herself, puffed her cheeks full, then let the air out slowly. She straightened and assumed a courtly bearing as we continued down the hall. "That is very cool," she said in her most refined voice.

We found our way to the main corridor that led to the club entrance. As we turned the corner, we saw a familiar figure. At the far end of corridor was Lorelei Rollings, clad in a racy black evening dress. She was moving swiftly toward the exit. If she had looked back, she would have seen us, but it was clear she was in a big hurry.

We stepped up our pace and reached the parking lot only seconds behind her. She had disappeared.

Scotts stepped over to the valet standing closest to the door. "My friend just came out," she said to him. "A beautiful, black-haired lady in a black dress? Did you see where she went? I wanted to say hi."

The young man nodded and pointed off toward a darkened corner of the parking lot. Meanwhile, I'd given my ticket to another valet and he'd dashed off to get my car.

After a moment scanning the lot, Scotts turned to the valet and pointed across the way, "Is that her over there, getting into the yellow car?"

"Ah, yes, ma'am, I think it is. That's Mrs. Rollings."

"Damn, I missed her. Who is she with? Do you know?"

"No, ma'am," the valet said, shaking his head. "She's usually with Mr. Rollings, but he. . . ah. . ."

"Yes, he died. I know. Thanks."

As it was, we didn't need his help identifying the driver. The car, a vintage yellow Cadillac, was forced to leave via the only exit lane on the lot. That lane ran not thirty feet from us. The driver was Jimmy Shyne. He was pushing to get them out of there as quickly as he could. Neither he nor Lorelei noticed us as they zipped by.

"You wanna?" Scotts asked, already knowing my answer.

The valet was there with my car a few seconds later. I pressed ten bucks into his palm and we hopped in the car.

"Let's go! They turned right at the gate," Scotts said. "And they're hauling it."

I wheeled it hard right.

"What the hell was Jimmy Shyne doing there?" Scotts asked.

"Who knows? Picking her up to give her a ride home?"

"Yeah, well, I never sit that close to *my* chauffeur," she said.

"So much for the grieving period."

"Three weeks is enough," she said. "You guys think we're going to miss you much longer?"

"You're all heart. Which way at this intersection?"

"I think we go right."

"I don't know about that – I didn't see which way."

"Take a right, then. Like I just said," she snapped.

"Hard to starboard, Captain."

I turned right onto a long, darkened street. There were no fading taillights to be seen. Empty as a church lot on Saturday night. I looked back and there was nothing that way either.

"We lost them."

"You know where she lives in town, right?" Scotts said.

"Good idea," I said and headed for the freeway back into Atlanta.

47

WE sat in the car down the street from the Rollings townhouse. Two hours had passed, the house remained dark. Clearly Lorelei and Jimmy Shyne hadn't been headed here from the Country Club.

"Want to head down to her other place?" Scotts asked. "We've got that spot I showed you, we can watch from there."

I looked at my watch, it was after midnight. It'd been a long day and fatigue was setting in.

"Not tonight, maybe—"

"You're right. We need to stakeout *both* places."

"I didn't say that."

"Not yet, but that's where you were headed."

"You know what I'm going to say before I say it?"

"It's a gift. Easier with some than others. Travis is easy as pie. You, mmmm, pretty easy."

"That's ridiculous."

"Aw, c'mon. Just trying to cheer you up. Ooooooh, I get it, you're ready to go home to Miss Moore."

"That's not it."

"You sure?"

"I'm sure."

"Because you don't sound so sure. . . uh oh. That little tiff the other day?"

"Not for discussion."

"Sure, okay. Just remember, I've been married, like, a hundred years and I know all the tricks – if you ever want to know how they're done."

I laughed. "There, I'm cheered. Let's give this a little longer, see what happens."

At five o'clock in the morning we were still in the car down the street from the Rollings townhouse. No sign of Lorelei or Jimmy Shyne or any other living creature for that matter.

Thank god for cigarettes. Otherwise I would have dozed off hours ago.

Scotts had sat bolt upright the entire time, eyes locked on the house. I wondered how she did it. I had known women who could remain on high alert for days on end. Without blinking. Without losing focus. How was that possible? I figured it was some kind of special vigilance gene women had.

I began fidgeting and Scotts looked over.

"I'm getting my second wind," I said.

"I don't know about this," she said. "May be time to give up the ghost tonight. What do you say?"

"Not yet. I need to talk to you."

"Oh?" She looked over with a touch of apprehension. "What about?"

"We need to sort through all this. I'm lost," I said.

She asked me *how* lost.

I told her.

"To begin from the beginning. . . Bobby Rollings was killed on Easter Sunday morning. That in itself, as you say, is odd. In the South, in the Bible belt, on the day of ultimate redemption? Who does that? Was it some kind of symbolic act? And that gothic funeral service, the preacher ranting, *This is the day the Lord has made.*   Did that sound like a taunt to you? A warning? Or, am I overreaching?

"And I can't shake this question: What does this story mean to Manship? It has some kind of personal meaning. Is it something about his dead brother? Or Lacobee? Or both?

"And what do I make of him sending me to Washington to meet this Gary Hooper guy? Who is Hooper, anyway? What's his role in all this? I've asked around the paper and he was Manship's right hand man back when Manship was actively running *The Democrat.* When Manship backed away, Hooper moved on to the *Wall Street Journal.* But even now, working for the *Journal,* Hooper refers to him as "the boss." Is my hunch right, was Hooper some kind of 'house intelligence' guy for Manship? Was Hooper assessing me for something like that? Or, to be fired?

"And don't look at me like that. You heard me, fired. Calvin told me I was on the PITA list – that's Pain In The Ass, in case you're wondering. Next step from there is the OTD list – that's Out The Door. But that's another story.

"Back to this one: Will Black. What the hell is he about? I know he alerted Manship to the murder. Manship told us he had lived in Latham County when he was a kid. Is that how he knows Will Black? What's the deal there? Why all the mystery? Will Black is following us, right? For our protection, he claims. From what? If there's so much danger looming, why doesn't he explain it? Is it the DA? The Sheriff? Lacobee? Big Cat? Who? Who the hell is the big dark demon?

"The biggest piece of the puzzle is the circle of characters surrounding the killing. Jacob Lacobee all but told us he killed Rollings. Came right out and said it. Dared us to catch him.

"But while I lean toward Lacobee, you like Lorelei for it. And I'll grant you, the woman's madness *is* compelling evidence.

"And we shouldn't forget the money motive. Her husband and grandfather hated each other. That may have, in her mind, put her inheritance at risk. If your grandfather was worth tens of millions while your husband was likely headed to the Federal pen, which boat are you climbing into?

"Still, to me anyhow, Lorelei is too crazy crippled to do it. Or even think of it."

"Now Big Cat, he's the wild card. He's a servant of two masters, beholden to Lacobee and at the same time has some kind of attachment to Lorelei. I saw love in his eyes that night he picked her up off the road. I know I did. There was a gentleness there you don't see from a man who is just wrangling a crazy woman at the behest of his boss. Jacob Lacobee hadn't sent Big Cat after her that night, that was Big Cat rescuing her on his own.

"It seems a fair bet, though, that if either Lacobee or Lorelei – either one – had asked, Big Cat would have willingly killed Rollings.

"But now there's Jimmy Shyne and that bunch. The Shynes have this arson-for-profit thing going, and maybe they're being funded by Bobby Rollings. I know from Hooper's notes that Rollings was dirty. He stole millions from some nuns, he sure as hell wouldn't have any compunction about throwing in with a bunch of arsonists.

"Manship thinks Jimmy Shyne isn't involved with Rollings or anything his gangster family is into. And yet, here we sit, waiting for Jimmy Shyne and Lorelei Rollings to return from an all-nighter.

"The business with Lacey is personal on the one hand, but I'm not sure her investigation of the Shynes isn't part of our story. I've known all along she was a career-first woman. We started out with that understanding, both ways. But after three years, she's become something more than a good source to me.

"But that's me, not her. And I think the breakup was a practical matter. As long as she and I were involved, and I was prying into the Shynes, her investigation was at risk. HER goddamn investigation was at risk. Hers! Believe me, if she saw it that way, that would be a deal breaker. And it would be *our deal* that was broken.

"Bitch." I slammed my hand on the wheel. I had to take a minute to calm down. Scotts stared ahead, stone still. I drew some deep breaths, several long ones.

"But. . . but, personal or not, I think *our* investigation and *her* investigation will converge, sooner or later. They'll converge. That's what I think."

I quit talking, stepped out of the car and lit a cigarette.

Scotts had sat in silence the entire time, listening carefully to every word I said. Some of it was new to her, some of it impassioned, some of it angry. I glanced into the car and she was still sitting motionless, eyes fixed on the Rollings place, probably wondering if I was losing my mind.

I stomped out the cigarette and got back in the car.

She sat quietly at least another five minutes, just to be sure I had nothing more to say. She was beginning to yawn regularly. She shifted uncomfortably in the seat and cleared her throat.

"Well. . . that *is* pretty lost," she said at last.

"And you're not?"

"Not that lost. But you know, there was a lot of that I didn't know until just now. Give me time to digest it, maybe I can catch up."

I chuckled. "Manship did say bring you along fast."

"That was pretty damn fast."

"Yeah, it was. So. Where do we go from here?"

"From here, I need to go home and get some sleep," she said. "I've got to. And now would be a good time to do that."

"I don't know. They've got to come sooner or later."

"No they don't," she said. "They've got other places. They may never come back. I'm exhausted. Another day, huh? What d'ya say, let's go. Run me to my car. It's at the paper."

"I know where it is."

"I wasn't sure. You said you were lost."

"I know where your car is."

"And you *really* sounded lost."

"I know where your damn car is!"

"Okay, okay. What a crab."

"I'm tired, that's all."

"Good. Me too. Let's go. To my car. At the paper."

"I told you – "

"Yeah, yeah, you told me. So let's move it that way, will you?"

"Be glad you didn't ride your scooter all the way up here tonight. Be glad of that."

"I could've handled it."

"No you couldn't."

"I damn sure could."

"No you couldn't. You're tired and bitchy. Never ride when you're like that. Never. You'll kill yourself."

"You're the one tired and bitchy," she said.

"All I'm saying is you don't ride when you're like that, you'll kill yourself."

"And all I'm saying is I'm the one with the damn gun, so let's go!"

"Okay, that's it," I said. "Done. I'm taking you to your car."

48

SIDEBAR:
"Twenty Years Down the Sunlit Path"

An Editorial by Adam Manship, Publisher
Excepted from: *The Atlanta Democrat*
April 4, 1988

. . . And yet, it has been only twenty years, to the day, since he was assassinated.

The Rev. Dr. Martin Luther King, Jr. will be remembered for many things but few more than his 1963 "I Have a Dream" speech – an address to over 250,000 people gathered on the National Mall in Washington on a sweltering hot August afternoon.

He had intended, by all accounts, to deliver a prepared speech on the "shameful conditions of race relations a hundred years after the Emancipation Proclamation." But a whisper to him from his nearby friend, the spiritual songstress Mahalia Jackson, changed the course of events.

"Tell 'em about the 'Dream,' Martin, tell 'em about the 'Dream!'" Ms. Jackson said, referring to an improvised riff she had heard him deliver before, in speeches to smaller gatherings. He heard her, set aside his prepared remarks, and told them about his dream.

Few could argue the significance of those remarks or the

man. Both would play a pivotal role in helping pass the Civil Rights Act of 1964, and then, in 1965, the Voting Rights Act.

Both that speech and that man have also had enormous influence on our black leadership today – including leaders like our own Atlanta Mayor Andrew Young and the many stirring young voices that follow him. We point specifically to young leaders like Cedric Fields, Harold Byonne, and Jimmy Shyne; and we gently remind all of Dr. King's bitter-sweet prescience: that his mission was "not an end, but a beginning."

This country *is* still beginning. In another "twenty years down the sunlit path of racial justice" – to borrow again from Dr. King – we will be discussing what today's black leaders have done for the country, this city, our citizens. We want to be sure today that all understand exactly what that discussion will cover.

It will cover what you have done about *your* dream.

49

OVER the next two days, Scotts and I reviewed our notes, went back to several sources for clarification, debated hunches, then hatched a plan of action.

She would press Will Black to find out why he'd introduced this new character, Ardis Cash. We knew he was a thug-for-hire but wanted to know what they were looking at him for in the Rollings murder. What did they have? A connection to the gun? To the car? To the Shynes?

She would also keep an eye on the comings and goings at the Rollings country place. She agreed she'd watch from a safe distance – from the spot she'd found earlier – and keep her distance regardless of what happened. She also agreed to shut down by midnight, no later.

At the same time, I would surveil the plantation and, from time to time, Lorelei's movements in Atlanta. That included keeping an eye on her townhouse and rolling past Jimmy Shyne's places of business once in a while.

We would touch base every day at 10 a.m. to compare notes.

Scotts drew me a crude map of Montrose Plantation and I saw that the best spot for my base of operations was the family cemetery, DeRussey. It was on the far side of Montrose, in a remote section of the plantation no longer in use. There was never a reason for anyone to go back there, Scotts assured me – except to bury bodies, of course. It was surrounded by dense trees and undergrowth and had back-door access – the trail that came in off FM 71, the trail Scotts had shown me earlier.

I figured I could get from the road back to the cemetery on my bike if it could handle the rugged, overgrown terrain. From there, I could follow the river a half mile or so on foot to a tree-lined levee. That would give me a concealed perch and a good view of the Big House.

Before my first trip, I put off-road knobbies on the bike, raised the forks for a little extra clearance and muffled the pipes. This wouldn't be the smoothest ride on the highway, but once I got on that trail, it would be sure-footed as a mountain goat. It would get me in and out quickly and quietly.

My first recon went off without a hitch. The trail back to DeRussey hadn't been used in some time, but it was clear enough to ride. Once at the cemetery, I found a dense thicket and hid the bike. I double checked my exit options then explored the place.

The cemetery was bordered by an ancient black-iron fence. At the south end was an opening and an arched header that read "DeRussey" in wrought iron letters. There was a foul odor coming from somewhere – I guessed it was the smell of a dead animal nearby, borne on the light breezes swirling around.

Near the center was a fresh mound of earth that must have been Bobby Rollings' grave.

I remembered that both of his parents were deceased and he had no siblings, but wondered if there was extended family somewhere. If so, did they know about this? There'd been no one at the funeral who looked like members of *his* family. Nothing but the Lacobees and locals.

Maybe Bobby Rollings wasn't the most admirable guy on earth, but there must be someone to speak for him. A cousin, an aunt, a grandparent. Someone to voice his side of the story. It would probably be an interesting one, come to think of it. One question I'd ask him: Why were you keeping your son from Jacob Lacobee? He wouldn't be answering that himself, now, but maybe there was someone – a distant relative or friend – who could. I made a note to inquire further then continued looking around.

Scotts had been right when she said there were a lot of graves in DeRussey. There weren't the "millions" she'd described – we might need to work on her sense of scale – but there must have been at least a hundred. Many were marked, some with granite headstones, others with crudely fashioned wood or brick markers.

There were a dozen mounds off in a far corner that had no markers at all. They were not identified as graves, but there was little doubt that's what they were. Were it not for their orderly arrangement, they likely would have gone unnoticed. Probably the intention. These must be the nobodies. The no-names.

As dark began to fall, I walked the half mile from the cemetery to the levee. I found ample cover among some young pines that had sprouted on top. From there, with binoculars, I could see the Big House and monitor traffic on the main drive.

I had marked a retreat, just in case, so I felt comfortable enough to settle in for an evening vigil.

Nothing much happened. At dark, Lacobee took the boy out to a tractor parked at the side of the house. They moved it into the large barn not far away. Big Cat rolled up soon after on another tractor, put it in the barn and went into the house. The upper south wing of the house, where Lorelei had her suite, remained dark, suggesting she wasn't there. By midnight, the house was totally dark, so I worked my way back to the cemetery, rolled the bike out and headed back to Atlanta.

For two weeks, we watched the Lacobees and Lorelei and exchanged notes. Lorelei, Scotts said, appeared to be readying her country house for sale. A realtor had visited twice, walked around the house taking notes and photos. A small van had come several times, each time hauling off pieces of furniture and antiques. Two men with a flatbed had picked up her husband's Mercedes sedan, leaving her with one car, the red Corvette convertible.

Once during that time Lacobee brought the boy to see his mother. Lorelei had walked out to meet them in the drive, had embraced her son, kissed him several times and talked with him briefly. Lacobee and the boy stayed less than fifteen minutes. Scotts was fairly certain that was the only time Lorelei saw her son in those two weeks.

There was a more frequent visitor, however. Scotts reported a "large, dark figure" slipping into the house almost every night. The visitor came afoot through the woods adjacent to the house – much the way Bobby Rollings' killer might have come – and was always still inside when she left her post at midnight. She was almost certain it was Big Cat.

Back in Atlanta, I observed Lorelei receiving a different visitor. Jimmy Shyne had been her guest at the townhouse on three occasions, arriving each time around 3 a.m. and leaving at sunrise. Shortly thereafter, she was off in her red convertible, headed south to her country home.

But I spent more time watching the plantation than watching Lorelei.

Lacobee seldom went anywhere on the grounds without the boy and Big Cat. The boy always rode with him in his big cultivator or whatever else he was driving. Every afternoon he and Cat would take the boy out shooting. By the end of the second week, the kid was getting good with the little double barrel .410 shotgun he carried. And he carried it like he knew what it was for.

In my third week of plantation surveillance, things livened up. I had been watching the place most of the day and as evening approached decided to make my way back out. I reached the cemetery with plenty of daylight left and was about to pull the bike from the underbrush when I heard rustling nearby. Then a burst of gunfire. There must have been a dozen shots. I slipped into the cover of the underbrush, froze, and listened.

In a few minutes, a tractor with a front-loader chugged its way into the cemetery. Big Cat drove and the boy sat beside him holding two rifles pointed straight up between his legs. The front-loader was filled with hog carcasses.

Big Cat rolled the vehicle up to a wide berm on the far side of the cemetery. There was a deep trench alongside. He squared the front-loader over the trench, pulled a lever and dumped the dead hogs. He and the boy climbed down and spread two bags of white lime over the carcasses.

They climbed back in and Cat turned the vehicle around to head back out. He paused for a minute before shifting gears and looked around. The boy turned to him anxiously.

Cat patted him on the shoulder and killed the engine. "It's nothing. That's where your daddy is," he said. "See that dirt pile, that's his grave. We was here for his funeral not so long back. You remember?"

The boy nodded.

"Papa will have a stone made up to put there. It'll have your daddy's name on it."

"There?" the boy asked, pointing at the mound in the middle.

Big Cat nodded. "He's in heaven, now. He's in peace for all of time."

The boy gave him a confused look.

"True enough. You look around you, all them graves are our family – yours and mine. All gone off to heaven to be in peace."

The boy looked toward the rows of unmarked graves and pointed.

"Those there you don't need to think about," Big Cat said. "Those are bad people. They did some bad things to us, and they ain't going to heaven. That's what happens. That's how the Lord works."

Big Cat suddenly stiffened and looked around. His eyes darted in every direction. He had heard something, or smelled something, or sensed something. That something might have been me.

"You sit here," he said to the boy in a hush. He took a rifle and stepped off the tractor. "I heard a nuisance in the bush. Shhhh, now."

He moved slowly and soundlessly toward the brush I was in. He chambered a round in the rifle. He eased closer.

I sat immobile, eyes trained on Big Cat. I was pretty sure he hadn't seen me yet and was hoping against hope he might still turn back. Suddenly there was rustling in the brush off to my left. I turned to face a wild hog rooting around not ten feet away. He was a big one, not quite the size of a cow but the biggest I'd ever seen. He saw me and started backing off. I made a quick jerk toward him and he scrambled out of the brush.

He went the wrong way. He moved into the open, right into Big Cat's sights. One loud crack from the rifle and the hog went down. He staggered back to his feet and began charging at Big Cat, blood spewing from the right side of his head. Cat unloaded three more rounds into the hog, the last one dropping him a few feet from his boots.

Big Cat drew the big pistol off his hip and put another three rounds into his head. He turned and walked back to the tractor. He climbed up without a word to the boy, handed him the rifle, then started the engine.

Within the next five minutes he'd scooped up the dead hog with the front-loader, dumped him in the trench, spread a bag of lime, and pulled out of the cemetery headed back toward the Big House.

When I could no longer hear the tractor, I eased up, pulled my bike onto the trail and pushed it all the way back to the road before cranking up. I got the hell out of there.

The entire ride back to Atlanta I thought of Lacey. I imagined she would be waiting for me at my place with a bottle of wine and a warm, welcoming embrace. She would smother me in comfort. But beyond that, beyond the wine and the warm embraces and all the comfort, she would simply be there.

She wasn't.

50

THE next morning, my phone rang early. It was Scotts, and this was urgent, she said. She wanted me to meet her that evening at her stakeout; it was important and she would show me when I got there.

I rode the bike down, planning to run back to the plantation after we met. I had my camera and wanted to get pictures of the unmarked graves. Big Cat had told the boy those graves contained "bad people." I wondered what his definition of "bad people" was. And who they might be.

If there was any truth to the rumor that DeRussey was some kind of killing field, we might be onto something. There had been such a case twenty years ago in Coweta County. Two dozen bodies of unidentified men, all murdered, buried in a farmer's field. It made national news. There was a book. There was a movie. The discovery of the bodies, it turns out, had begun with a rumor.

Scotts was already in place when I arrived shortly before dark. She had pulled her bike off the road into the shadows of a small stand of pines. She had an annoyed look in her eyes and anger in her voice.

"Will Black is being dodgy," she said. "Something's going on. Sheriff Fowler is finally back in town and he's taken over the investigation. And the DA – that lazy ass. . . do you know he hasn't tried a case in twenty years? Anyhow, the bastard's issued a gag order to every cop in town – serious gag order, serious consequences. Will Black knows something about Ardis Cash, but now he's clammed up."

"Someone's turning up the heat."

"Looks like it. But this is what I want you to see. You say you haven't seen Jimmy Shyne at Lorelei's place in several nights?"

"Right. But I haven't been there every night."

"That's because he's been down here every night this week."

"When does he get here?"

"Right after dark."

"How the hell's he doing that when he's got a bar to run?"

"I don't know, but it's him. In his yellow Cadillac. You'll see."

She was right. Shortly after dark we saw headlights creeping down the road to the Rollings house. As it turned into the drive, the headlights went off. There wasn't much of a moon, but enough to let us see it was a yellow Caddy. A figure slipped out of the car and ran into the open front door. Not ten minutes later, two figures came out the front door and hurried to the car. They were moving fast, and there were trees and distance between us, but we were almost certain it was Jimmy Shyne and Lorelei. Who else would it be?

I turned to Scotts who was already pulling on her helmet. I grabbed mine.

"You think you can ride that thing without the headlight?" I asked.

"Eyes like a bat," she said.

"Okay, nice and slow," I said. "I'll lead. We follow the taillights."

We did that for a couple of miles, but at a main junction, the Caddy surprised us. Instead of turning right, back toward Atlanta, it took a left, south toward Montrose Plantation. We were able to keep eyes on them for several more miles until they took a quick turn onto a small road leading back into the woods. I pulled over and let Scotts catch up.

"Where does this lead?" I asked.

"Looks like it goes back to the plantation. Into the west side. I'm not sure. I don't think I've seen this turn before, it's hard to tell."

"We need to turn the lights on if we're going any further," I said. "Dense woods down there, no light on the road."

"Let's roll. If anybody asks, we're night riders. No law against that." She switched on her headlight. "You follow me for a while."

She pulled away without discussion.

We wandered the back roads a good thirty minutes, clearly lost and without a sign of the yellow Caddy or any other traffic. We came to a junction that Scotts recognized. She raised an arm and pointed left. As we proceeded down that road, the terrain began to look familiar. So did the fence line. I wasn't sure exactly where we were, but I'd been here before.

As we rounded a sharp bend, we saw taillights a half mile down the road. It looked like it could be the Caddy. And though it was moving, it wasn't moving fast.

Scotts slowed and I did the same. We kept our distance and continued to follow the lights for another mile of tight turns. As we hit a stretch of straightaway, the car gunned it and the tail lights disappeared into the darkness. We sped up but couldn't seem to catch up. Scotts must have had her throttle wide open. I was struggling to stay close.

We had to throttle down as we came through a tight turn. There was a sharp rise as the turn straightened and we had to jump back on the throttle to climb the hill.

I had closed to about fifty feet of Scotts when I heard the first shot. Her bike wobbled wildly then spun out of control and threw her across the road into a ditch. I squeezed on my brakes and was able to slow up before I slammed into her downed bike. The impact tossed me into the thick grass on the side of the road. I felt a thump in the gut as I hit the ground but knew instinctively I wouldn't be hurt badly. I looked up and saw Scotts a few feet away. She was moving, but slowly.

There were more shots; they tore into the bikes.

I crawled to Scotts. She'd gotten her pistol out of her jacket and was ready to start shooting back. I moved up beside her and tugged her down into the ditch, into the deepest cover I could find. She raised her gun in the air and opened fire, sending four or five rounds into the night.

With no real idea where the shots were coming from, and looking into pitch darkness, she may as well have been shooting at the wind.

Whoever was shooting at us, though, had plenty to sight in. The headlights of both bikes were still on; the bikes were sitting ducks. The rounds continued to come our way, every other one ripping into metal. I figured a shot was going to hit a gas tank any second. That would throw some light on things.

Abruptly, the shooting stopped. But it wasn't for anything we had done – Scotts had stopped firing minutes earlier. We listened and heard nothing. No movement, no car starting, no road noise, no nothing.

Then we heard the siren. It wasn't far, and it was getting closer. In a half minute, we saw a flashing blue light topping the rise and headed down to us at high speed.

I rolled closer to Scotts to see what kind of shape she was in. She looked dazed but was breathing steadily. She looked toward me, glassy eyed.

"Oh, shit," she whispered.

"Are you hit?" I said.

"I don't know," she said weakly. Her eyes began to flutter. "My head hurts pretty bad."

Then she lost consciousness.

51

By four a.m. Scotts was on the non-critical list and resting quietly in room 323 at the Atlanta Trauma Center. Her husband, Travis, sat in the room with her while Mr. Manship and I sat in a small waiting area down the hall.

It had been Deputy Weaver who had appeared on the scene moments after the shooting stopped. He had quickly assessed our condition, saw I was unhurt and that Scotts appeared to have a head injury. He called for an airlift to the Trauma Center, and once Scotts was on her helicopter ride, drove me in.

He told me he'd been on routine patrol when he heard all the shooting. When I seemed to reject that story and thanked him for following Scotts and saving her life, he reiterated: "I was not following anyone, I was on routine patrol."

"However you happen to be there, thanks," I said. But I knew, and he knew I knew, he'd been out that way by design – by Will Black's design.

Weaver had called Will Black on the way to the hospital and filled him in. Will Black said he would be there first thing in the morning and wanted me to wait for him.

Mr. Manship had arrived at the hospital only moments after Weaver dropped me off. He'd immediately called his personal physician to look in on Scotts and the doctor was in the room with her now.

Having said little since he arrived, Mr. Manship turned to me and breathed a heavy sigh. "This is one of the best trauma centers in the world, but I want a second opinion. David Haynie is the best."

"Yes, sir," I said.

"Will Black informed me, you know," he said.

"Yes, sir. I figured that."

"We will not let anything happen to her. Enough is enough."

His eyes flickered anger and there was an emotional quiver in his voice I hadn't heard before. The fedora he always wore sat at a slight tilt on his head, as if put on carelessly, hastily. He drummed his fingers rapidly across his knees as we sat in the stiff waiting room chairs.

After a short time, the doctor came out of Scotts' room and stepped our way. Mr. Manship stood as he approached, I followed suit. The doctor spoke directly to Manship.

"Lucky girl, Adam," he said. "Nothing too serious. A concussion that she should get past in a few days. There are some lacerations, mostly minor – road rash from skidding across the pavement I'd guess. She'll get stitches and be sore for a while, otherwise she's okay."

"She wasn't shot?" I asked.

"No bullet holes that we could find," he smiled, then offered a nod of assurance. "She'll be fine, she will. Feisty little thing, too. She's already lobbying to get out. But to be safe, I want her to stay here a couple of nights. She's going to hate it, but she needs to do it. They'll stitch her up, watch the concussion and infections, and keep me in the loop. It's a good crew here."

"Thank you, David," Mr. Manship said. "Sorry to call you out in the middle of the night."

"I haven't done this in a while. I miss it a little. But only a little."

They nodded, shook hands and the doctor started away.

"Can we look in on her now?" Mr. Manship asked.

"Not yet. Give her a day to rest."

Mr. Manship and I took our seats again in the waiting area. He said he wanted to wait for Will Black. Meanwhile, he had questions for me.

"Who was it?" he asked.

"Scotts thought it was Jimmy Shyne and Lorelei. We both did. I'm not sure, now."

"So who?"

"I don't know. I want to say Lacobee, but I can also see Lorelei mixed up in it somehow – even though the two of them are at open odds. I know you don't think Jimmy Shyne is involved, but….I don't know, it all happened so fast….I haven't quite gathered my thoughts."

"You do that while I go make a few calls. I'm going to have our head of security put a man at her door. Probably unnecessary, but let's do it anyway."

"Yes sir. That'll make her husband feel better."

"How is he with all this?"

"I think he's…okay. I'd guess he's long ago resigned to the fact that she does what she does for *her* reasons, not someone else's."

"Don't we all?"

He stood, said he'd return in a few hours and asked me to wait for him right where I was.

I stretched out on the sofa in the waiting area and had finally dozed off when I was shaken by a hard kick in the foot. Lacey Moore stood hovering over me. Her face was smeared with a scowl. This didn't look like a sympathy visit.

"This is why, asshole," she hissed. "I warned you. I told you you were in deep shit and you didn't hear me. *This* is what happens!"

I rubbed my eyes, hoping this was a nightmare. It wasn't.

"Didn't I?" she said, her voice ratcheting up from a hiss to a shriek, her eyes widening.

"Yes, Lacey, you did. You did, damn it. But you know, when everyone keeps warning me away from everything, it makes me curious. A fatal flaw, I know, but that's me."

"I'm happy you're so fucking self-aware," she said. "Because this is *all* you. You almost got that girl killed, and you have damn sure screwed up my case. You're barking up the wrong tree with the Shynes. They have nothing to do with your story."

"You see, that's a perfect example. When everyone keeps pushing me away from somebody – like, say, Jimmy Shyne – it draws me to them."

"Like a moth to the flame. You know, you just do not get it. You've spooked every fish in the pond. How the hell do you think I know about this – about you and the girl nearly getting killed? How did I get up here this morning? Who do you think told me? The word is out. Everywhere. You don't see what a mess you're making? For you and for me? You don't see that?"

"I think I do, now you put it that way."

"What is it? What exactly do you see?"

"Someone different. Someone different from the woman I thought I could love."

She shook her head in disgust. "You are an impossible fucking moron." She glared a moment longer then stomped away, her shiny black high heels driving into the tile floor, clanging like spikes into rock.

It was possible she was right, I *was* a moron. For instance, I had no idea how she knew about the shooting or how she got to the hospital so soon. The word was out, she'd said. Who did I think told her, she'd asked.

Moron me, I had no idea. But now I was curious.

52

Two hours after Lacey had stomped away, Will Black showed up. It was about eight a.m. He came lumbering down the hospital corridor, stopped for a minute to talk to the security guard Manship had posted, then moved on toward me in the sitting area. When he had my attention, he thumbed me to follow. He turned and headed back out of the hospital.

His squad car was sitting in the circular drive at the main entrance. Mr. Manship sat motionless in the front passenger seat. Somehow I wasn't surprised to see him there. Will Black signaled me into the back. As I climbed in, I saw I'd be sharing the seat with three shotguns and two ammo crates full of 12-guage shells.

He pulled out of the hospital grounds and was up on the freeway headed south in a matter of minutes.

The two of them sat silent in the front seat, eyes fixed ahead. After a while, my curiosity got the best of me and I asked where we were going.

"To the crime scene," Black said through the heavy wire screen that separated the front seat from the back. "Pick up the motorcycles, for one."

"We were lost when the shooting started, I don't know where we were."

"I do. Did you know you were on Lacobee's plantation?"

"We were lost, following the Cadillac. I thought we were on a public road."

"It is, technically. But Lacobee owns both sides of it for miles in either direction. So he likes to think of it as his own."

"I've noticed that about him," I said, and slumped back in the seat. I rubbed my temples and closed my eyes. My head was pounding from no sleep the last 24 hours and a half-dozen cups of coffee the last two. My back was getting stiff and sore from my roll off the bike. I was in a wide-awake-but-fuzzy-headed-hurt-all-over haze.

I had looked in on Scotts just before we left. Travis was asleep in the chair beside her bed. She was stretched back, eyes closed, head slightly raised. I only got a peep at her through the door before a nurse ran me off, but she appeared to be resting well.

I couldn't help but think that this would be the end of our short partnership. Travis seemed like one of the most easy-going souls in the world, but everyone has their limits. In truth, I couldn't blame him if he drew the line right here. This wasn't good. When I heard the shot and saw Scotts go flying across the road, it scared hell out of me, and I've been in some tough spots. Lacey was right, this *was* a mess.

At the same time, and as I'd told Mr. Manship earlier, I didn't think there was any person or thing that could stop Scotts once she had her mind set. She was dogged. And damn fearless. She had pushed me aside so she could take the lead in that last stretch of our chase before the shooting. That was her. That's where she wanted to be: Out front, leading the charge. They call that "hero ball" in sports. When people start firing guns at you, though, it's not all that sporty.

"Tell me what happened," Will Black said, snapping me out of my moment of reflection. I looked up and saw we were still on the freeway headed south. We had another fifteen or twenty minutes before we'd be in Latham County. "From start to finish."

I recounted the night, from our stakeout, to the shooting, to the hospital. I ended by adding that Deputy Weaver had probably saved us, being nearby as he was. That drew a blank response from Will Black.

"So you're not sure it was Jimmy Shyne's car?" he asked.

"That's right. I am *not* sure it was his car. Something about it looked different. I think. But I'm not sure. And the taillights we were following right before the shooting. . . I'm not sure that was even the Caddy."

"Helluva an eyewitness you are. But you *are* sure it was Lorelei the car picked up at her house? You're sure of that?"

"Had to be. We'd been watching her place since before dark. A little after dark – around nine o'clock I think, the yellow Caddy rolled into the drive, lights off. The driver went in, ten minutes later two people come out, get in the car and go, we follow. If it wasn't Lorelei in the car, I can't imagine who."

"A lot of speculation in all that," Black said.

"You sound like a lawyer."

"I been bit by enough of them to know what they like to chew on."

Manship turned back to me and spoke for the first time since we'd left the hospital. "Based on everything you've seen and heard and know, you think it was Lorelei in the car? And you believe whoever was in that car was shooting at you?"

"Yes, sir. I don't see how it could be otherwise."

Manship turned to Will Black and waited for his response.

He didn't take long.

"I'll have to go talk to her as soon as we finish at the scene."

53

THE three of us stood looking at the two motorcycles – a tangled mess on the shoulder of the road, right where they'd fallen last night. There were a half-dozen bullet holes in each, a testament to the marksmanship of whoever had been shooting at us.

The moment was a study in contrasts: The warm spring morning light falling into this quiet pastoral setting, the air cool and crisp, still fresh with the smell of dew – and three beleaguered, angry men standing there staring at a bullet riddled heap of metal, the ire seething inside each one apparent in their strained faces.

Will Black circled the wreckage slowly, peering down here and there for a closer look. Mr. Manship and I stayed back near the car as he'd instructed.

After a survey of the wreck, Black moved back to us. He scratched his ear and was about to say something when we were startled by a sound. It wasn't much of a sound – just the faint scrape of feet on the road – but it was moving closer.

Will Black reached in the car and grabbed the shotguns. He handed Mr. Manship one and offered me one. I took it.

We listened and watched.

Just up the road from the wreck was a rise then a sharp turn. The shoulder and roadside were overgrown, thick enough with trees and brush to make it a blind turn. That must have been how we'd lost the car last night. It had topped the hill, rounded the turn and stopped abruptly. Then the driver, or both, had jumped out and opened fire.

The approaching steps grew louder and in a moment came over the rise and into view. It was Jacob Lacobee and his great-grandson strolling down the middle of the road. They were both armed with double barrel shotguns, tilted down, breeches open.

Lacobee appeared to be as surprised to see us as we were to see him. He stopped, threw his arm out and stopped the boy. He looked at the three of us, taking a moment to eyeball us one by one, as if he could see into our heads and assess our intentions. He turned his look to the wreckage and again appeared to be surprised.

"What's this all about?" he said to Will Black as he and the boy stepped a little closer. They came within fifteen feet and stopped again. "This is my land, you know."

"This is a Latham County road, Mr. Lacobee," Will Black said. "We had a little trouble out here last night."

"Is that right?" He nodded slowly, his eyes trained on Will Black. "Trouble, you say?"

He turned his gaze to Mr. Manship and tipped his hat. "And what brings you out here, Adam? A little trouble, too?" He eyed the shotgun Manship was holding. "You come out here to take care of something your ownself, Adam?"

Will Black jumped back into the conversation. "Nobody's taking care of nothing but me. I have to investigate this wreck. There was a shooting here last night."

"Was there now? We didn't hear no shooting up to the house."

"No sir, but if you take a look at those motorcycles there, you'll see there was."

Lacobee glanced over at the bikes then back to Will Black. "Wasn't none of us. We're all quiet, peaceable folks. We was all right there at home, sound asleep."

"Well, there was some shooting, and I think Lorelei might be able to tell us something about it. I'm gonna need to talk to her. You know where she might be this time of day?"

"I 'spect she's at her house, asleep in her own bed."

"I'll need to go wake her then."

"No you won't, Will Black. She won't be talking to you. She'll be talking to the Sheriff, if he needs her to. Not you. I don't trust you to use good judgment when it comes to my family. I think you got something against us, some kind of. . .what do they call it nowadays?. . .prejudice, that's it." He looked down at the boy, put his hand on his shoulder and asked him: "You ever heard that word, son? Prejudice? That means they don't like us. Don't know why, but they sure don't."

"No sir, that's not true," Will Black said.

"And as for Adam, there, I got no idea what ever got into his craw, but he's hated me for a lifetime. Half a century or more, ain't it Adam?"

Mr. Manship looked at him long and hard before he said anything.

"You know what it is, Jacob."

"No, I don't, Adam. I might could guess, but I can't say I know for sure."

"You and Louis."

"Yeah, that's what I thought. Never have understood your hatred for me in all that."

"You had to have your eye-for-eye, didn't you, Jacob?"

"No, sir!" Lacobee shot back sharply.

"You, or one of your own, shot him dead, left him laying in the creek for me to find. Like you tried to do right here. I have no doubts any more, Jacob."

"No, sir!" Lacobee screeched louder.

Abruptly, the boy snapped his breech closed and leveled his shotgun at us. Lacobee reached over and pushed the gun down. "No, boy. Open that gun back up right now. This ain't no time for shootin.'"

The boy did as he was told but kept his eyes fixed on Manship.

"Adam, you're mistaken about this here. About all that back then, too. You must be forgetting things. Your brother was a friend of mine. And nobody never shot him. He disappeared. He ran off after he killed my little brother with that tractor. I know it wadn't purposeful, but he done it nonetheless. Then he got scared and took outta here. Louis ran, Adam. I oughta know, I helped hunt him for a week. Nobody never found him. Your mind done slipped on all that."

Will Black stepped forward, inserted himself between Manship and Lacobee. "I have to get about my business here. I need to get photographs, do a search of the road and get this mess cleaned up. We need to break this up."

"You telling me to leave, Will Black? Cause me and the boy was going out shooting nuisances. And we gotta go this way to get to 'em."

"No, sir, I'm not stopping you. You go on about your business as you need to. I'm just telling you we're gonna be busy on this stretch of road for a little while this morning. We need to block it off. Then you can have it back."

"I see. Well, we can be accommodatin', can't we, son?" He grinned, reached down and took the boy by the hand. "This is a county road and you go ahead with your county business. We can cut across this field here and get right to where we need to go."

Before he left, he took one last look at Manship. "Adam, I know I still owe you a dove hunt. You never once accepted my invitation in all these years. Why don't you come on down when you're ready, we'll go kill us something."

He touched his hat then he and the boy headed off across the field.

"Where is he headed?" Manship asked Will Black as they watched Lacobee and the boy disappear into the distant tree line.

"That will take them back to the Big House," he said. "He may not be done with us."

Will Black quickly took photos of the wreck then told me to get anything off the bikes I wanted to keep. He and Manship talked quietly while I gathered the tank bag off Scotts' bike and the saddle bags off mine. He signaled me to throw them in the trunk. Mr. Manship listened intently as Will Black told him something, then he climbed back into the car, took up his note pad and started making notes.

Will Black radioed for deputies and a tow truck and then asked me to walk up to the top of the rise.

"Keep an eye up and down the road and back that way toward the plantation," he said. "I don't think the old man's that crazy, but I been wrong about crazy before. Run on up there."

The reinforcements – three deputies in patrol cars and a tow truck with a two-man crew – arrived shortly. The cops immediately began searching the area. It looked like they found shell casings, but I couldn't be certain. It took the boys on the tow truck some doing to get the bikes onto the flatbed. I could tell by the twisted metal and dangling parts they were both totaled.

As I kept watch over the next hour, I considered what I'd heard. These were new pieces to the puzzle. Manship believes Lacobee, or one of his kin, killed his brother, Louis, fifty years ago. Lacobee says that didn't happen, that his brother ran away, fled in fear after killing Lacobee's younger brother. But what Lacobee actually said was "Nobody never found him."

An interesting choice of words, I thought.

I heard a sharp whistle and saw Will Black had cleared his crew out and was signaling me back to the car. I had just started his way when we heard a gunshot in the distance. I looked back down the road then out across the fields. I saw nothing. Will Black hustled up to me.

"Sounded like a shotgun, from over there across that field, beyond the trees," I said. "Hard to tell for sure."

We stood and listened a couple of minutes more. Nothing.

"That's bullshit they didn't hear shots last night – so quiet you could hear gnats fuckin' out here," he said. With a smirk he added, "Guess he and the boy found their nuisance."

He turned and moved back toward the car. "Let's get you two back, then I'll go talk to Lorelei."

Before we reached the car I stopped him.

"What's Mr. Manship doing here?" I asked.

"He insisted," Black said. "He said 'Enough is enough.' That's all I know."

"Yeah, well, about that. . . I need to show you something," I said.

"Not now, " he said impatiently and opened his door. "First things first."

He cranked the car while I hurried around to the back door and jumped in. I hadn't got the door fully closed before we were speeding off. Mr. Manship never looked up from his note pad.

54

B<small>Y</small> the time we left the site of the shooting, it was noon. We'd been there almost three hours, and I realized I'd been awake for almost thirty. The thought of all that lost sleep made my head pound – your psychology becomes your biology as they say. The rest of my biology wasn't doing so well, either. My ribs were aching from the toss off the bike and the pain in my right wrist was beginning to feel like a small break or a large sprain. I prayed for the day's drama to be over so I could get some sleep.

My prayers were apparently not being heard that day.

As we turned off the main highway onto old Highway 37 – a shortcut Will Black said would get us over to the Interstate faster – we saw a bright yellow car approaching at high speed. It had to be doing a hundred. It roared past so close we all three held our breath then exhaled relief.

Will Black recognized the driver.

"Jesus H., that was Lorelei! I gotta slow her down."

He jammed the brakes and spun the car in a one-eighty swirl of black smoke and flying gravel. The car fishtailed then squared back up on the highway. Will Black gunned it. We were in pursuit of Lorelei and the same yellow Cadillac Scotts and I had been following the night before.

"That the car?" Will Black asked.

"Looks like it," I said.

"Let's see if the blue slows her down," he said and flipped on his lights and siren.

It didn't. The driver of the car, if it was Lorelei, was either impervious to the cop car chasing her or she was just plain ignoring it. She was moving so fast through the turns we couldn't try to close the gap between us and have any hope of staying on the road.

As she neared the entrance to the plantation, we thought she would slow for the turn into the main gate. She roared past it. A half mile later she slowed for a long sweeping curve, then midway through took a hard left onto a narrow blacktop.

Will Black slowed and followed. He killed the siren and the lights and slowed even more. He was going to hold back, see what she did.

"Where does this go?" Mr. Manship asked him.

"Back to the foreman's place."

"She's going to Big Cat's?" I asked. "I thought he lived at the Big House."

"Don't know if he stays here, but these are the foreman's quarters down this way," he said.

"Didn't you say Cat and Lorelei were close as kids?" I asked.

"Appears they still are," he said with a half-twisted smile.

The road was overgrown, the passage so narrow the high weeds and brush scraped the sides of the car. We slowed to a crawl, but the yellow Caddy pushed ahead. It was soon out of view.

Will Black was amazed and amused. "That woman is so goddamn crazy, she's got no idea we're back here. I guaran-damn-tee you she never heard the siren, never once saw the lights. Not once."

Further in, the road began to widen, open up. The shoulders slid smoothly off into open fields, many with fresh turned dirt ready for planting. Ahead, and off to the right, a narrow hard-packed drive ran thru a cattle gate back to a circle of oak trees. In the shadows of the oaks was a small wooden cabin. A tractor sat off to the left of the cabin. The yellow Cadillac was parked to the right, up near the front door. Lorelei was getting out of the car and tip-toeing toward the door, as if to surprise who was inside.

Will Black turned down the drive and eased toward the cabin. We watched Lorelei tap softly on the door. By the time she'd tried three times with no response, we were close enough to hear the taps. Will Black killed the engine and rolled down his window.

How Lorelei did not hear us approaching was a mystery to me, but she never looked back. She turned the knob and pushed the door open slowly. She peeked around the door as she inched in and then, in an instant, came reeling back out, half-stumbling, half-running in horror, screaming at the top of her voice.

Will Black threw open his door and bolted toward her. Mr. Manship and I jumped out and followed.

She fell to the ground on her back and began flailing legs and arms wildly. Her screams were so loud they could have been heard a dozen miles away.

Will Black reached her first and bent down to pull her up. She kicked him in the head – though it looked more accidental than purposeful – and continued screaming and flailing.

It took some doing, but after a moment of tangling with her, the three of us had her upright, somewhat quieted and gasping for air.

"Can you hold her a second?" Will Black asked us. "I need to take a look."

We nodded and each took an arm. She looked at me and recoiled with a shriek. She spun away into Mr. Manship, who caught her in his arms. She grabbed onto him, pressed her head to his chest and closed her eyes. She held on tight, sobbing.

Will Black gave me a wave and I followed him to the cabin. He pushed the door open slowly, with the back of his hand. We took two steps in and saw it: The nearly headless body of Big Cat sitting in a wooden spindled chair in the middle of the room. Blood covered his chest and the wall behind him. A pump shotgun laid on the floor at his feet.

"Jesus H. Christ," Will Black said to himself. He shook his head and continued to stare at the body. What was left of the head was slumped forward showing a gaping hole in the back. I was struck by how the body was still sitting upright, hadn't toppled to the floor. Then I saw the belt strapped across the front of his chest and buckled to the back of the chair.

Will Black saw the same thing.

"Seen a suicide do something like this once," he said. "Coroner thinks it's because they don't want to leave a mess for their loved ones to clean up. Don't know I believe that, but never heard a better explanation."

"You think this is suicide?"

"Well, it's supposed to look like one, ain't it?"

"That shot we heard back on the road?"

"Could be. The blood's still wet. C'mon, let's get the girl back to the car. I need to call for help."

Mr. Manship had already managed to walk Lorelei over to our car and sit her in the back seat. Will Black got on his radio and called for deputies and the coroner. That done, he moved around to the passenger side of the car and climbed into the back seat with her. She was beginning to breathe steadily and trying to blink her eyes into focus.

Once he established she was clear-headed enough, he had questions for her.

"Is that your car you're driving, Lorelei?"

"It's Big Cat's. He got it not too long ago."

"What were you doing in it?"

"I. . . I drove it home last night after. . .after we came out here for a while."

"To his house? You came to his house last night?"

She nodded. "Then I went home. I was supposed to come get him this morning." Her breathing was getting shorter, more labored. Her eyes were washed in tears. They were pouring down her face. She was trying to continue but was losing her voice. "I was late. . .so I. . .I tried to hurry. . . I thought he was in trouble. . . I. . . " Her eyes began to flicker, then they snapped shut. She slumped over into Will Black's lap.

He sat motionless for a few minutes then slipped out from under her and got out of the car. He took off his brown jacket, made a makeshift pillow and slid it under her head. He gently closed the door and came around to the front of the car where Manship and I stood.

"What a mess," he said to no one in particular.

Mr. Manship eyed him carefully and said nothing. It was clear from the past few hours that he and Will Black had some kind of strong relationship, some established common ground. Not that they were fast friends or relatives or business associates – rather they had some kind of bond that suggested common experience and mutual regard. Mr. Manship was ten or fifteen years his senior, so it seemed unlikely they'd been pals in their youth. But however they were connected, and as unlikely as the pairing might seem, there was an exchange of understanding between them that was strong and firm.

Within ten minutes, Deputy Weaver rolled up.

"Coroner said it'll be an hour or so," he called to Black as he walked over. "O'Con and Johnson are on their way."

"You get any sleep, Weaver?" Black asked him.

"Yes sir, enough."

"Good. The Sheriff coming?"

"We couldn't raise him, Chief."

"What a surprise. Let's go inside and see what we got." He looked at Manship and I and gave us the nod to follow. "You can come in but not far. And do not touch."

Once inside, Will Black started taking photos. Weaver did the same. He'd take a photo, bag an item, label the bag and then take it out to the porch to get it out of the way.

He examined the shotgun carefully and identified it as a Remington twelve-gauge pump with the plug out and five or six rounds of buckshot still in it.

"Don't screw with it, Weaver," Will Black said after he saw the deputy stick his finger in the end of the barrel looking for any gunshot residue. "We know it's just been fired. Put the safety on, wrap it up and take it outside. Then get over there and get pictures of that back wall, all that spatter."

While Weaver took pictures of the blood patterns, Will Black circled the body in the chair, slowly, several times. It seemed he found the whole scene a little too stagey for comfort. A little too suspicious. In fact, he said so several times. But moments later he would reverse himself, say it was pretty clear Big Cat killed himself. Mr. Manship stood near the door the entire time, motionless, eyes fixed on the two cops, soaking in the scene like a sponge determined to get every drop.

In the kitchen area, Weaver found a woman's purse.

"I'm pretty sure this ain't the big fella's, Chief. What should I do with it?"

"Look inside, Weaver. I'd say we got probable cause, wouldn't you?"

"Yes, sir."

Weaver dug into the purse and found it was Lorelei's – her driver's license and credit cards stuck in a wallet. There was also a big roll of cash. Looked like nearly ten grand, Weaver said. And pills, no prescription.

"Got something else, here, Chief," he said as he held up a business card and read from it. "Ever heard of a nightclub called *Erebus*? In Atlanta? Jimmy Shyne, Proprietor? And look who's name's written on the back…a friend of ours, Ardis Cash. Kind enough to provide us his phone number, too."

Will Black had moved over to the kitchen to take a closer look at the contents of the purse when we heard footsteps scampering across the porch. Immediately after, there was a car door slam and a roaring engine.

Black was first to the door and saw the yellow Cadillac tearing away from the house, back toward the cattle gate.

"Goddammit, she's running!" he shouted. He stepped onto the porch, looked around and turned to Weaver. "Where'd you put the shotgun?"

"Right there, Chief," he said. "I leaned it outside the door, right against the wall."

"She's got it and she's gone. Let's go. Weaver, stay here and wait for the coroner. And don't touch another thing."

Lorelei reached the cattle gate as one of the deputies turned in. She charged straight ahead, ran him off the road into a ditch and kept going.

It wasn't O'Con, it was another deputy. He jumped out of the car, saw Will Black waving him over and ran toward us.

"Johnson, you stay here with Weaver," Will Black shouted to him. "Call O'Con and see where the hell he is! And try the goddamn Sheriff again. And the DA."

Manship and I followed Black as he scrambled to his car. He looked at us as he opened the door. "You're gonna have to come with me, I can't leave you here."

We got in quickly. Black said nothing as we roared through the gate, down the narrow road back to the highway. Manship took a glance over at him from time to time, but likewise said nothing.

Saying nothing, though, wasn't my style. "Where is she going, Chief?" I asked from the backseat.

"I don't have to think twice about that," Black said as he yanked a hard right turn up onto the main highway. "She's going to her grandfather's place."

"Why would she do that?" I asked.

"Hell if I know," he said. "Maybe he's the only one left to kill."

55

WE sped through the plantation gate into a swirling trail of dust just beginning to settle on the drive. That meant Lorelei was only a minute or two ahead.

Boyd O'Con had caught up with us out on the highway and was now right behind. Chief Black killed his flashing blue lights and O'Con did the same.

As the Big House came into view, we saw that the yellow Cadillac had plowed across the lawn and rammed into a small cluster of crepe myrtles. The driver's door was wide open.

Lorelei had climbed out of the car and was now waving the shotgun she'd grabbed back at the cabin. She was shouting hysterically toward the house.

"You killed him, you bastard, you killed him!"

She stumbled forward a step or two and fired wildly at the front porch. The shot shattered the beveled glass window in the front door and sent splinters of wood flying. She screamed again and fired another wild shot, this one shredding the wicker porch swing.

Will Black eased closer, to within fifty or sixty feet of her, and started short-blasting his siren. She heard it this time. She spun toward us, leveled the shotgun toward the car and fired. We dove into the floorboard.

We were far enough away the shot missed. Will Black peered over the dash, told us to stay down, then drew his pistol and slid out of the car. He crouched behind the open door. O'Con leapt from his car and hustled up beside him, staying low.

Jacob Lacobee stepped through the shattered front door with a double barrel shotgun at the ready. He stood tall and fearless and looked right at Lorelei.

"What the hell are you doing, girl?" he called.

"You killed Big Cat! For no reason at all, you just killed him," she screamed and fired a shot at him. He flinched his left shoulder like he'd caught a pellet or two, but the heart of the shot hit wide of him. His shoulder dripped blood.

"You're crazy, girl, damn crazy," he barked.

Will Black lifted his pistol skyward and fired two warning shots. Lorelei spun at him and fired again, this time hitting the front grille of his car.

"You leave me alone while I kill him," she yelled at Black. "That's all he wants to do is kill everybody I love! That's all! Kill, kill, kill!"

Will Black dropped his aim lower, but still well over her head, and fired another warning shot. "Put that gun down, Lorelei."

She lifted the shotgun and took careful aim at him. She pulled the trigger but got nothing. She had emptied the gun.

She turned back to Lacobee and did the same thing. She yanked at the trigger violently several times, getting nothing.

Lacobee pointed his shotgun over her head and fired. She whirled to Will Black and pointed her gun at him. He fired another shot over her head.

She turned back to Lacobee, then spun back to Black, then back to Lacobee, then back to Black. She was spinning in mad circles, a whirling dervish with a shotgun.

Lacobee fired a blast into the air and yelled, "You stop that, girl! Stop that right now!"

She dropped the shotgun and bolted across the lawn toward the adjoining cotton field.

Will Black and O'Con started after her.

Lacobee threw down his shotgun, raised his hands and started down the steps of the porch, calling after them.

"Don't hurt her! Don't hurt her, Will Black! You know she's crazy as a betsy bug!"

Lorelei didn't get far into the field before her feet got tangled in the rows of young cotton sprouts and she fell flat on her face. O'Con managed to get to her ahead of Will Black. He pulled her to her feet and without cuffing her started her back toward his patrol car.

When they got to the lawn in front of the house, Lacobee rushed to her. Will Black stepped aside and let him reach for her, pull her into his arms. He clutched her tightly, with all the love in the world. Her face, turned up on his shoulder, was caked in a mask of tears and dirt. Her eyes seemed to have gone dead.

After several moments, Will Black told Lacobee he'd have to take Lorelei into town. Lacobee clung to her, as if he hadn't heard a word the Chief said. The pair stood there, rocking slowly, the sound of her whimpers and cries coming and going.

"I have to take her in, Mr. Lacobee," Black said again. "We'll get her to the hospital first, have her looked at, be sure she's okay. I can let you—"

"You're gonna take her right there to the Sheriff's Office, that's where you're gonna take her, and that's where you're gonna keep her," he said.

"Where she goes will be up to the Sheriff and DA, but for now we have to—"

"That's right, Will Black, it ain't up to you. And I'm saying that's where she goes and that's where she stays for a little while til we can get all this settled and she can come back home. That's what."

Will Black said no more. He gently took Lorelei's arm. O'Con got on the other side, took the other arm. They half-walked-half-carried her back to O'Con's car. They eased her into the back seat, buckled her in and closed the door. Will Black said something quietly to O'Con as the deputy got into his car. O'Con nodded, did a U-turn and slowly pulled out. Lorelei stared blankly through the window as they rolled away.

Will Black watched them off for a second then stepped over and picked up the shotgun Lorelei had thrown down. He motioned us back to his car. As we pulled away, Jacob Lacobee climbed the front steps heavily, hand pressing the wound on his left arm. Eva Lacobee stood in the remains of the front door, her face in her hands.

56

IT was midnight. Sleep was not coming for me. The image of Big Cat's body – nearly headless, slumping but still upright, strapped into a small wooden chair in the middle of a blood soaked room – the image would not go away. Superimposed was his face, his very much alive face, deep black eyes filled with passion, with sadness, with heartache for Lorelei as he lifted her in his arms that night on the road. Her face would not leave my mind either – the face of a woman, a beautiful women, so beautiful and alluring and yet so childlike, so unable to apprehend anything that was happening to her, or that she made happen; that beautiful face smeared in dirt, washed in tears, clinging so desperately to her grandfather; that child of a woman, wrapped in the arms of the person she had just tried to kill, her eyes absent even the vaguest comprehension. And the boy, that child of hers, now Lacobee's – what kind of hell had he fallen into?

It was two a.m. I had been without sleep for over two days.

When Will Black dropped me at my apartment that afternoon, he had warned: "Get in there and go to bed right now. You're sleep deprived. Worse than being drunk. Bad things happen if you let it go too long. I've seen it. Bad things."

It was happening. Right now.

Sleep deprivation feels like hell. It feels like the first time you realize you have sinned. You find it hard to believe, then impossible to believe; your entire body goes numb; while your eyes do close, they keep dancing. You wonder, why are they dancing? How are they dancing when the joint is closed and the lights are off? They dance behind closed doors, in the dark? Is that it?

Sleep deprivation can make you do foolish things. But disoriented as I was, I knew better than to call Lacey. It was too late to call Scotts in the hospital. Calvin was off duty and by now stewed. My dad was. . . my dad was dead ten years now, but he would have had an idea to help me sleep. No, come to think of it, not even he could do that tonight.

Sleep deprivation *does* make you do foolish things. And floods your mind with questions. Questions that may never be answered. What in the hell was that between Manship and Lacobee? Their stories are so crossed. SO crossed. Manship's brother, Louis – was he dead? Alive? Did Lacobee shoot him as Manship says or did he turn tail and run as Lacobee says? Come on, Louis, what happened? Have you seen what's going on here? The carnage? Bobby Rollings, Big Cat, Lorelei, Scotts? What the hell, Louis? What happened, man? Are you part of the carnage, too?

Sleep deprivation does not necessarily make you sleep. It impairs decision making. And it, along with several beers, can make you do very foolish things. Like calling a lost love – who lived with her new husband in Baltimore – in the middle of the night to tell her how your personal life was falling apart, that you were in way over your head at work, that you were nearly killed by a sniper, *again*, and that you know you were a damn fool for walking out on her five years ago.

Fortunately for foolish people, there are tolerant angels.

And there was one who lived in Baltimore, who listened to me patiently and kindly for at least three hours that night until I fell asleep with the phone in one hand and a half-finished beer in the other. This angel, herself a journalist when she was not tending to whining souls from her past, also reminded me of a key investigative tool I had apparently forgotten.

"Why don't you go look it up?" she said.

I was awake by mid-morning; I'd had just a few hours sleep but that would keep me going a while longer. When I was clear-headed enough, I called the hospital. Travis said Scotts was resting and doing fine, but she was asleep. I told him I'd check back later.

I called the archivist at *The Democrat.* We had the most complete news archive in the State of Georgia. I asked her to search the years 1925 to 1935 and pull anything she could find on the shooting death of a teenaged boy with the last name Manship; and also pull anything in that time frame on the death of a young boy with the last name Lacobee. Both in Latham County. She told me to give her an hour, then call back.

When I did, she had found nothing. That didn't mean they didn't happen, she said, but the paper *was* covering Latham County at the time. Sorry, no story there.

The State Records Archive – located in the world's ugliest building just a short drive down the freeway in Morrow – *did* have a story to tell.

There was a death record for a Samuel Lacobee, age 6. It was recorded in 1932 in Latham County. The coroner's finding was "accidental death." The boy had been hit by a tractor after wandering out onto a farm road near dusk. The driver of the tractor, Louis Manship, 16, had been moving the tractor in from the field and had not seen the boy. No charges had been filed.

There was no death certificate anywhere for a Louis Manship.

It took several hours and the help of a records clerk who wouldn't give up, but I finally found something worth the dig. There had been an application for *Declaration of Death of Louis Manship* filed eight years after young Lacobee's death. The application had been made by the parents of Louis Manship, Augustus and Sylvie Manship. It stated that Louis Henry Manship had disappeared in May of 1932 and had not been seen or heard from since. Law enforcement documents from local and state police supported the application. The documents described two official searches for him, one conducted immediately after his disappearance and another some time later. Neither yielded any trace of him.

Because seven years had passed since he had been seen by anyone – a statutory requirement for such a declaration – the application had been granted. Louis Manship, though his body had never been found, was legally dead.

Now we had a new mystery. The stories I'd heard from Lacobee and Manship didn't jibe. Mr. Manship had said he'd found his brother laying face down in a creek, shot in the chest, and that he and his father had buried him. Jacob Lacobee's story was actually closer to the facts I found. He had said that Louis Manship had killed his younger brother, albeit accidentally, then disappeared.

Jacob Lacobee, it seemed, had been right.

He also had a private cemetery with two dozen unmarked graves.

It was late evening before I made it to the hospital. I'd called Scotts' room twice more during the day and both times had been told by Travis that she was doing fine but was unavailable, she was talking with her doctor. It wasn't that his voice was nasty, he just didn't sound all that pleased to hear from me.

In some ways, I was dreading the visit. I was certain that either Travis, or Scotts, or both, would be telling me she was done. That she had to quit, this time for sure and for good. By the time I'd arrived, though, Travis had left the hospital and gone back to New Bethany to attend their two children. Scotts was sitting up in the bed, dressed as if she were ready to walk out the door.

"About time," she said.

"Where are you going?" I said in my most cheerful voice. "Got a date?"

"Very funny. I'm getting out tomorrow morning and I do have a date, as a matter of fact. A date to kick Jimmy Shyne's ass from here to kingdom come. You should see what he did to me. I've got cuts and bruises up and down both sides. They hurt, too, dammit! I'm going to show him what we mean by 'country justice.'"

Her face went flush. The vitals monitor she was connected to started blinking and beeping.

"Okay, take it easy. It wasn't Jimmy Shyne. Calm down, let me explain."

In time she did, and I told her the whole story: The rush to get her to the hospital; Will Black and Manship and I meeting Lacobee out on the road; the three of us chasing Lorelei in the yellow Cadillac and finding Big Cat dead in his cabin; Lorelei trying to kill her grandfather and us; and finally, Lorelei's arrest.

"Damn! Where's Lorelei now?"

"In jail. Will Black took her in."

"And it was Big Cat's car we were chasing, not Jimmy Shyne's?"

"That's what it looks like."

"But Big Cat's dead? Really? Lorelei didn't – did she?"

"No. No way. She was genuinely horrified. She wasn't play-acting on that."

"Damn, I missed the best part," she said. Her mouth and eyes drooped in disappointment.

"Some, but there's more. Only…"

She cocked her head in that weird angular way she had of expressing annoyance. "Only what?"

"I assumed you were done."

"What do you mean, done? Do I look done?"

"Well no, but I assumed you'd be resigning because of. . . because of all this." I swept a wide gesture around the hospital room.

"You mean because someone was going to make me resign? Is that what you mean?"

"Not *make* you exactly, but. . ."

"I see. Well, you can forget that because I've had a talk with both of them, Travis and Daddy. And with Mr. Manship, too, who at least came to see me today, unlike other people I work for. And you know what he said? He said, 'The more you fear, the more fear finds you.' That's what he said."

"I buy that."

"So, I'm not done. Not quitting. Ain't scared. Nothing. Same as before. Same, same."

I was stunned and relieved. This was good news. Scotts was good, *very good* at this work, and she would only get better.

"So shut up about that and start talking about something interesting." She laid back in her bed. "You said there was more, so tell me. I've got nowhere to go right now."

I told her in more detail about the meeting on the road between Mr. Manship and Lacobee. There were contradictions in their stories – maybe it was their memories, who knew? But State Records seemed to support Lacobee's version.

And then there were the unmarked graves at DeRussey.

"Oh, yeah, I found out where that comes from, by the way," she said, sitting back up. "The Latham County Clerk of Court told me – he's kind of our local historian. He said back in the 1850s a few French settlers came up from Louisiana and homesteaded. One of them was Antoine DeRussey. All of his son's died in the Civil War, but afterwards, his only daughter married a man named Jacob Lacobee. That was the great-grandfather of our present-day Jacob Lacobee. That's where the plantation started, and that's why that old cemetery is there and they call it DeRussey."

"However it got there, it's got unnamed bodies in it."

"And so you're wondering. . . let me see if I can guess," Scotts said. "You're wondering if Mr. Manship's brother is buried in DeRussey. Right? The Lacobees killed him to avenge the killing of the young Lacobee boy, then dumped the body in their secret graveyard. Is that what you're thinking?"

"More. . .wondering."

"And, that *would* be a good story. It would explain Mr. Manship's interest in Jacob Lacobee, and in the Rollings murder. But how would you confirm something like that?"

"That's the question."

"It is," she said. "Lucky for us, that question is not going anywhere. So why don't we set it aside for the time being and get back to Bobby Rollings. Is there anything new on that? You say Lorelei's in a psychiatric workup and will be charged. But, at worst it'll be charges of, what, shooting at cops? Something like that, whatever that's called. Not for killing her husband. So, there's still that. Who did that?"

"You're right. And…" I pulled out my notepad with a small flourish and flipped to a page I'd dog-eared. "And, we're back to Jimmy Shyne – but not so you can go murder him. So he can tell us about Ardis Cash. The same guy Will Black gave us the photo of – the one he wanted you to show the Rollings kid. Remember that? Well, the name Ardis Cash turned up on the back of Jimmy Shyne's business card, found in Lorelei's purse, in Big Cat's cabin."

"Jimmy Shyne here we come!"

"Exactly. And I got this from my guy at DMV – a bill of sale from Jimmy Shyne to Ardis Cash for the Cadillac. Why is that important, you may ask."

"Why is that important, I ask."

"Because according to my guy, they undervalued the car by about twenty-five grand," I said.

"Jimmy Shyne basically gave a vintage Cadillac to Ardis Cash."

"And why would he do that?"

"Let's go ask him!" she said. "Hey, you want to go now?"

"Ah, no, I don't. And you don't either," I said. I looked at my watch for emphasis. "It's almost midnight. They're releasing you first thing in the morning. We'll go then. Can you wait that long?"

"Okay," she said. "Okay. But, hey, what about the bikes? Travis said he thought they were goners."

"DOA, both of them. We'll have to get new ones. And I've got the money for that in my hip pocket."

"You got the money? From where?"

"Guess."

"The Man?"

"If you mean the boss, yes. He gave me some cash some time back, said I'd need it. He okayed this yesterday."

"Oh, I love him, don't you?" She smiled a dreamy smile and pressed her hands together in a prayer pose. She eased back in her bed slowly, pulled the covers up to her chin and closed her eyes.

"You going to sleep in your clothes?" I asked.

"I might. Get out of here."

I rose and watched for a moment to be sure she wasn't faking. She lay quiet and still, listening for me to leave.

But I wasn't ready to leave. I had one more thing.

"Operation Frequent Wind, 1975," I said quietly. "We were pulling our troops out of Saigon and evacuating as many as we could. I was on the media unit covering it and still a raw recruit, just six months duty. Two of us talked the Sergeant into going to the front, 'for the real story, the award-winning photos.' He shouldn't have listened, he knew better. We had clear orders to stay at the rear. But we pushed and pushed, wouldn't let him say no. We got into downtown Saigon, it was bad. Very bad. A sniper's bullet grazed me, hit my buddy square in the chest."

Her eyes lifted slowly open. "Your buddy. . . you. . . you lost him?"

"Yes."

"That scar?"

"That's right."

She closed her eyes and fell silent for a moment. Then she looked up.

"Me being here isn't your fault," she said softly, evenly. "Not your fault."

She closed her eyes again. She pulled the covers tighter. "Now get out of here, big day tomorrow."

I turned the light off at the door and stepped out.

57

WE were sitting in Jimmy Shyne's office when he strolled in a little after nine a.m.

"Sweetlips!" he said when he saw Scotts rise to greet him. He threw both arms open wide. "I knew you couldn't stay away."

She took his right hand and shook it formally. "Good morning, Mr. Shyne. Emily Scott, and your remember Gil Coates, *The Atlanta Democrat.*"

"Ohhhh. My heart's broken. You mean this is an official visit, not a call for love?"

"Maybe another time," she said with a polite smile. "Can we talk to you privately, in your office? It's important."

Jimmy Shyne studied her a moment. He looked over at his receptionist, June, who had invited us to sit and wait for him. She gave him a slow, affirming nod.

"Sure," he said. "Anything for the press. Come in, please. Happy to see you both."

He swung a gesture toward chairs in front of his desk as he circled to his large executive chair behind it. "Please have a seat."

I took one of the chairs. Scotts remained standing and waited for him to settle in. On the way over, I had suggested that she take the lead. I'd noticed in our first interview that she had a way of making him antsy, throwing him a little off his game. Why was anybody's guess, but mine was that he got distracted by his own fantasies of him and her on that big couch in his office.

Scotts had happily accepted the role.

"Mr. Shyne," she began matter-of-factly, "we know about your many nights with Lorelei Rollings – who is now in jail, if you did not know it. And we know that you are acquainted with the man they call Big Cat – who happens to be dead, in case you did not know that.

"We also know that before being dead, Big Cat was driving a vintage yellow Cadillac – the same Cadillac you sold Ardis Cash three months ago. But maybe *sold* is not the right word, because you *gave* it to him at a price about twenty-five grand less than its value. Sweet deal for him.

"We also know your father reported one of his shotguns – a valuable one from his prized collection – stolen just a week before it was used to kill Bobby Rollings. Interesting, so far?

"Last, but not least, we know that your father, your uncles, your brothers and sisters and every cousin you have from here to the Atlantic seaboard are under investigation for a big time arson scheme that might just send that entire little empire up in smoke. But, do you know what?"

"No...what?" he said carefully. His apprehension was obvious in his frozen stare, his tightly pinched lips.

"We don't care! And do you know why?"

"No idea."

"Because we don't think – or rather our boss doesn't think – you are anything but at worst an unwitting puppet, or, at best, plain unlucky to have been born a Shyne. Now, my partner and I, on the other hand, maybe we don't see it that way, but the boss is called the boss because...he's the boss."

"And he's always right."

"Exactly."

James L. Wilson

"That's all very interesting," he said. "But I'm still wondering why you're here, Sweetlips?"

"Because we have the deal of the century for you, Mr. Shyne."

"Oh, good, I love good deals."

"Like the deal you made with Ardis Cash on the Caddy?"

He shrugged. "Yeah, not my finest play. But there *were* circumstances."

"And that, Mr. Shyne, is exactly what our deal is about. Those circumstances. You tell us everything about them, totally off-the-record, for Mr. Manship's ears only. He's got no interest in your sorry morals or your petty crimes. Am I right, Mr. Coates?"

"You are," I said.

"What he is interested in is candor. And he will deeply appreciate yours, right here, right now. And, of course, down the road.

"And if you have any question about how much Mr. Manship's appreciation is worth – which would be a stupid question, but this is after all *you* we are talking about – go ask Mayor Young.

"So, there's the deal. What do you say?" She went silent.

He stared at her still as a stone, transfixed. I thought he was dead right there in his chair. He let out a long breath to indicate he wasn't.

"Man, that was some pitch, Sweetlips! Would you like to work for me booking bands? Some of those goddamn agents I have to deal with could use a good ball-bustin' like that."

"No." She said to him. She turned to me and put on a sad face. "Looks like I blew it. No dice, Coates. Let's go."

"No, no, Sweetlips! I wasn't sayin' no. I was tellin' you how much I admire your persuasive powers." He walked over and opened his office door. "Junie, you go ahead and take your coffee break now. Make it thirty minutes. Down in the cafeteria. Lock the outer door when you leave."

He closed the door and returned to his desk. He waited until he heard the outer door lock before he said anything.

"Sit down and relax, Sweetlips. I have a story for you."

Scotts threw me a wink and took the chair. We both pulled out our notepads and pens. Shyne cocked his head and gave us an alarmed look.

"Your name will be nowhere in these notes," Scotts said. "As soon as we report this to the boss, we burn them. Fair enough?"

He nodded and began his story.

"Lorelei Rollings came to me one night, several months ago at the club. She was high flyin' on something. Out of it. She needed someone to do her a nasty favor, she said. I told her what I tell anyone: The nastiest man I know is Ardis Cash. That's all there was to it. Never another word from her about it. I doubted she even remembered asking."

"Ardis Cash?"

"He's the go-to brother for bad times down in the ward. So they say. Not that I would know first hand. Big Cat's dead you say?"

"Yes."

He looked to me. "What happened?"

"Shotgun to the head. Seems to be a rash of that," I said.

He shook his head as if to say he wasn't surprised. "Figured he was in for a big letdown. Maybe not that bad, though. Cat was crazy over Lorelei. Loved her all his life, he claimed. He told someone at the club that he was her 'first' and she was his 'first,' back when they were kids."

"You believe that?"

"Yeah. Yeah, I do, actually."

"Go on," Scotts said.

"Not too long ago, he started referring to her around the club as his 'lady.' Problem was – besides the fact she was married to Bobby Rollings – Big Cat wasn't her 'man.' Not her exclusive man, anyway. There were others. Many others."

"Did you make all those introductions?"

"No, no! I'm no matchmaker! But our club is a social club, you understand, and that's what's supposed to happen there."

"A social club, Jimmy?" Scotts said.

"Sure, baby. We're Uptown, don't you know? Nothing but high class people, high class entertainment. Do you know I almost got Michael Jackson there once? True. Michael Jackson, almost!"

"As they say, almost only counts in hand grenades and shotguns," Scotts said. "So, they were all patrons of your club – Lorelei, Big Cat and Bobby Rollings?"

"Members."

"Excuse me, *members*. How often did the Rollings visit?"

"Very. Lorelei and Bobby – neither one of them could get enough playtime. For him, it was anybody – man, woman or whatever. For her, mostly men, and there were always plenty available."

"Present company included," Scotts said.

He threw his hands open and looked to me. "What can I say? You've seen her, man. How's a brother to turn that down? I couldn't."

He turned to Scotts. "I'm sorry, Sweetlips, I admit I was a little wild before we met. Now my heart's pure."

Scotts had been wearing a poker face but had to crack a smile at that. I did, too. Jimmy laughed loudly.

"Why did you sell Ardis Cash the car so cheap?" she asked.

"I dunno, maybe I had something else on my mind that day. I was campaigning back then, you know."

"No, no. No BS, Jimmy, seriously. No BS," she said.

"Right, right. Yeah, you're right. The simple truth is, we lied on the bill of sale. He paid me what I was asking in cash but wanted to cut the sales tax – which is very high here in Georgia, by the way. Too damn high. But I can always use the loss for taxes, so I agreed. And that reminds me…you know we turn some heavy cash down there at the club, Sweetlips, so keep that in mind when you're thinking about me. I'm *always* flush!"

He was beginning to have a lot of fun with his flirtation bit. She ignored him.

"Simple as that? The pettiest crime in the world?"

"The word petty doesn't do it justice. *Embarrassingly* petty. You can see why I didn't want to tell."

"How did Big Cat end up with the car?"

"No idea. But the story I hear is Ardis has got himself in a mess. Something about some fires down in the Fourth Ward – and before you say anything, hand on the Bible, I don't know any more about that. You can go ask the DA – your lady, there, Miss Moore – I told her everything I know. I'm not in that business. I'm legit, one hundred percent. There may be Shynes in all that mess, I'm not one of them."

"So Ardis Cash needs cash to get out of town, so he sells the car?" Scotts asked.

"Could be. But it seems like Ardis was driving it the last time he was down at the club. That was. . . I'm not sure. . .two weeks ago, maybe three? Maybe before the killing."

"So, if I understand, this is the story you're telling: Ardis Cash *might* have been hired by Lorelei, and he *maybe* killed Bobbie Rollings. Then he *for sure* gets his ass in hot water for some arson jobs and he decides he's got to get out of Atlanta. To finance his departure, he *maybe* sold Big Cat his yellow Cadillac. And then, of course, *maybe* killed him. How does any of that make sense?"

"I don't expect my people to make sense, Sweetlips. That would be one crazy-ass expectation. But, like I say, Ardis Cash is the nastiest man I know. Everybody else knows it, too. Hell, even the cops know it and they're the last to know anything around here."

"I find all this hard to believe."

"There, you see what I mean about crazy-ass expectations!"

"Okay, okay, I get it." She looked over to me. "What else do we want to ask him?"

"One more question," I said. "Who do you think had Bobby Rollings killed?"

"I was wondering when that was coming. And you know, I honestly don't know and don't care. No, I do care, a little, because he was a big spender down at the club. Otherwise, that's an Uptown problem, and I could care less."

"Do you have any idea who might have pulled the trigger?"

"No idea on that, either, but I know who didn't."

"Well, that's something. Who *didn't*?"

"None of the people we've talked about so far."

"None of them?"

"Hell no. There's way too many stupid niggers around here who'd do that job for a few hundred. Now, one of your suspects may have set it up. But I can guarantee you whoever did is so layered up by now the cops will never figure it out."

"So, whoever did it is home free. That's what you think?" Scotts asked.

"Well, Sweetlips, let's just say I think there's better odds of that than of you and I ever falling in love."

She chuckled as she stood. "You have a rare gift of insight. Thank you for your time. We'll tell Mr. Manship how helpful you've been."

As we started out the door, he added: "You know. . . that Rollings woman, she really *is* crazy. And I don't mean just crazy, I mean *crazy* crazy."

"And men love that, do they Mr. Shyne?" Scotts asked him with a devilish grin.

"Oh yeah, Sweetlips, we do. We *really* do."

58

Jimmy Shyne had talked a lot but said little we didn't know. For instance, we already knew we didn't know who killed Bobby Rollings. Scotts was convinced Lorelei knew who did. She was less convinced that Lorelei was behind it. She wanted to find her and talk to her again.

Scotts had a growing sympathy for Lorelei, a suspicion that far from being a criminal, she was the victim of a dark undertow, some strong, silent pull of fate she couldn't even see much less escape.

I suggested it might be her own miserable instincts that got her where she was. Scotts didn't care for that view and spent the next three days determined to find her.

Lorelei had to be in New Bethany somewhere – either in the hospital, or the small psych unit there, or the jail. It seemed likely Will Black knew exactly where. But he was suddenly nowhere to be found. That alarmed Scotts.

She tried everything to get in touch with him, including having her father call his home. No answer. She ambushed her cousin, Boyd O'Con, in the courthouse parking lot, but he was tight lipped. She tracked down Deputy Weaver, figuring if anyone would be willing to help, he would – after all, he'd saved her life a week earlier. He, too, was mum.

"Judge Whitaker's orders. I cannot talk to anyone about the Rollings case or about anyone connected with it. None of us can," Weaver told her.

And where was Chief Deputy Black?

"I couldn't say," Weaver said.

I, meanwhile, had to see Lacey, whether she liked it or not. I caught her at noon in the courthouse, in the hallway just outside Criminal Courtroom B. The place was bustling with her colleagues scrambling for a lunch break, so I figured she'd have to remain civil.

"Yes?" she said, stopping in front of me, clutching case files to her chest. "What is it?"

"Two things, Lace, and it won't take a minute. Give me one minute."

"That's about all I have," she said.

"Okay, one, we no longer believe that Jimmy Shyne has any part in the Fourth Ward fires. Are we right to leave his name out of our stories?"

She considered the question a moment. "You would be wise to do that," she finally said, hardly moving her lips.

"Two, and this isn't even a question, I just need to say it: That day in the parking garage, that hit-and-run attempt was for you, not me. It wasn't some drunk driver, and it wasn't for me, and you know it. If Jimmy Shyne had nothing to do with it, it was the Shyne family warning you to stay away from their golden boy. That's what it was."

She arched an eyebrow. "Was it now?"

"That's what I think."

"Well, it worked."

I must have looked dumbfounded. Or plain dumb. Whichever, she relaxed her stiff pose and smiled sympathetically. She asked me to follow and we stepped from the main hall to a side corridor. The corridor was empty. She leaned against the wall.

"Come closer," she said. "I don't want to have to shout."

I moved very fast, very close. Close enough to kiss her.

"Hey, close enough. Back up a step."

"What the hell are you doing, Lacey?"

"My nighttime voice. I want *you* to hear this, and nobody else."

"I love your nighttime voice."

"I know you do. Now listen. I've been pulled off the case. They shut it down."

I started to say something and she put her fingers to my lips. "I said listen. I don't have forever to explain. Maybe later. Suffice it to say somebody big enough to have the State AG's ear wants us off the case, so we're off."

"How do you know that?"

"I know that because my boss told me, and then he picked up all *those* files and gave me a desk full of new ones. It wasn't that hard to comprehend."

"Yeah, but shut down? What about Jay Plummer, and Thames and– "

"Dammit, Coates, listen. I'm good with it. We're *all* good with it. Happy, in fact. When you're done with your deal. . .when you're done, maybe I can tell you more."

She leaned her face in close – close enough for me to breathe in that lovely *eau de Lacey*. She held it there for a moment then whispered, "Nighttime voice, now: See you later. Bye."

She stepped away and disappeared into the busy hallway and the rush of events.

Needless to say, my spirits were lifted. It felt like Lacey and her icy heart were thawing. But my suspicions were raised. She had confirmed what Mr. Manship said weeks ago, that Jimmy Shyne wasn't the bad apple, he was just from a bad bushel. But the arson investigation was shut down? When they already had so much? I had never seen anything like that. And did that mean the DOJ investigation was shut down, too? I had come to see the two as probably connected, that one had opened the door to the other. Now, were they closing both doors?

I hurried back to the paper and put in a call to Gary Hooper at the *Wall Street Journal*. I got his desk. Or what used to be his desk. I was told he was in Kuwait setting up a news bureau there. The fellow I talked to, George Bradley, told me he'd taken over Hooper's files. When I told him who I was and asked about the DOJ investigation Hooper was working, he knew exactly what I was referring to.

"That story fizzled," Bradley said. "DOJ shut it down for some reason, no idea why."

The Shynes had dodged the bullet. Somebody had major stroke.

Two hours later Mrs. Christian called me for a meeting with Mr. Manship. That night, the usual time, the usual place.

I rang the bell promptly at nine, and Mrs. Christian promptly answered. She led me to his office. He was in his usual leather chair smoking a cigar and making notes on the pad in his lap. He waved me over.

"How's our girl?" he asked, setting the notepad aside.

"Her old self, sir. Back in the field already. She's trying to track down Lorelei Rollings. Also trying to learn what the disposition of her case is. But we can't get in touch with Will Black. Everyone down there is under a gag order by the judge."

"Will Black will be back on the job tomorrow, you'll be able to talk to him then."

"Good. I'll let Scotts know."

"It might be better if you made the call."

"Yes, sir, I will."

"Nothing mysterious here, Mr. Coates. I asked a favor of him and he has been taking care of it for me. I imagine he was happy to get a couple days away from all that down there."

"Yes, sir. That was – still is – some mess."

"Isn't it? So, tell me. . .I'm sure you have questions. What would you like to know about all this that I can tell you? There are still holes in our story, I expect."

"Yes, sir. We are getting close to knowing who killed Bobby Rollings. And why. That was the precipitating event, you know, the story you originally sent me out for."

"Yes."

"But in the process – and I know you understand how I couldn't help wonder: Why this small town murder? Why the veil of secrecy? What's your interest? I know that's a lot of wondering and none of my business– "

"Jacob Lacobee."

"Yes, sir, that became obvious the other day."

"I believe he killed my brother, or knows who did, and I've been watching him every day since. Simple as that."

"Yes, sir. And the business about your brother disappearing?"

"Lies, nonsense, I don't know which. He's an old man. It doesn't matter. I found my brother's body, a bullet right through his heart. I helped my father dig his grave back of the field. My father knew, and I knew the Lacobees did it. No charges ever filed, but we knew it."

"That was fifty years ago?"

"Something like that. More I think. I know, that's a long time to be lugging something like this around. It's one of *my* life's solemn issues. I only have a few, that's one of them."

"Yes, sir. . . I, ah…"

"Do you have another version of events?"

"No. No, sir. I was just clearing that up in my own mind."

"All clear then?"

"Yes, sir. Clear."

"We all do it, Mr. Coates – imagine events and circumstances for our own convenience. And that's the difficult line we face, the one between what we imagine to be true and what is true. But as our friend Flannery O'Connor reminds us, 'The truth doesn't change according to our ability to stomach it.'"

"I like that."

"She was one of our own you know, Miss O'Connor. Born in Georgia, spent her life here, a newspaper woman for a time. She would be my age now, had she lived."

"Did you know her?"

"I did. Fairly well. Mrs. Scott reminds me of her in many ways – much the same constitution, those two. There have been others over the years. But Mrs. Scott gets it – I like her. We have a place for her."

"Yes, sir."

"You haven't asked about Mr. Hooper."

"No, sir. But I did learn today that he's in Kuwait setting up a bureau there. He'd told me when we met that would be happening."

"He will be there for years, I expect. I wanted him to meet you, because I wanted him to tell me if you were ready to take over the work he's been doing for me."

"I see."

"I started this business, I'm afraid. As a board member of Georgia Commerce, I was skeptical of Bobby Rollings' dealings with the Shynes from the get-go. More than skeptical; I saw what he was doing. I talked to him about it. Rollings didn't seem to care. I don't know what he thought, but he was a contentious little shit. So I gave Hooper some information, asked him to walk it down to Justice, see what they thought."

"And they took it."

"They did. Never pick a fight with a man who buys ink by the barrel, as Mr. Twain said."

"But now that investigation has been shut down," I said.

"That's what I understand. Win some, lose some."

He paused for a moment. His cigar had gone out and he wanted to relight it. Plus, I think he wanted to give me time to absorb all he'd said. After a couple of vigorous puffs, he turned my way with a twinkling eye.

"This is such a good cigar. Are you sure you won't?"

"No, sir. Thank you, though."

"Mr. Hooper thinks you're ready. Do you?"

"If he thinks I'm ready, and you're ready, I'll give you everything I've got."

"I would like to put Mrs. Scott with you. Make it a team, you at the head. I expect you'd rather work alone, but I think you could complement one another. Could that work?"

"Yes, sir. I can adapt. And she's very good."

"Fine. Let's do that, then." He tamped out his cigar then clapped his knees with his hands. "Let's call it an evening, shall we? I'll have Mrs. Christian see you to the door. I think you have a busy day tomorrow."

"Yes, sir, I do."

I said good night and Mrs. Christian ushered me out.

59

I was on the phone to Will Black the next morning, asking about Lorelei.

"She's right here in my jail," he said when I finally got a call through. "The DA had to charge her with something, so he's going with attempted assault."

"On a police officer?"

"Nope. Civilians were there. Attempt was on them. Wink, wink."

"That's it?"

"That's it."

"Why's she still in jail? Didn't Lacobee bail her out?"

"That's the strange thing. One of many. The DA asked the judge to deny bail and order a full psychiatric exam, both at the request of her family."

"The judge went along?"

"He and Lacobee are Deacons at the First Baptist, hunting cronies."

"Where does Lorelei go for the psych eval?"

"Nowhere. The doc comes here."

"And Lacobee?"

"Here every day. A couple of hours, sometimes. Brings the boy once in a while. Again, judge's orders."

"That's some setup. A kept pet, he gets her out to play with when it suits him."

"That's the system," Black said.

"Screwy system."

"That's only for starters. These two take the cake. On the judge's orders, they get a private room for their visits. All we have here is the interview room, so we set them up there. Now, I sure as hell ain't supposed to, but I do it anyway – I watch. The hell of it is, they know I'm watching – at least the old man does – and he could give a shit. In their own world, those two. You wouldn't believe your eyes."

"You're not talking some kind of, like, conjugal visit?"

"Hell no, son. That would almost be understandable compared to what goes on between those two."

"Any way I can look in?"

"No, sir. No way. I'm already on the outs with the Sheriff and DA. That's all they'd need."

"Think about it, Chief. Help me out here. We're on the same side."

"Figured you'd play that card sooner or later."

"I have to ask. My boss is a don't-take-no-for-an-answer guy."

"I'll think about it. How's the girl?"

"She's okay, she's good. She didn't quit – still with us, still full of piss and vinegar."

"Our own Nellie Bly."

"Tougher than she looks. I'll let her know you're back in the saddle, she can stop by. She still has questions for you."

"Don't do that. Not now. Got that gag order, we can't talk."

"That didn't seem to shut you up just now."

"Son, you breathe a word of this conversation, I'm a goner."

"Sure, sure. I was joking."

"Sometimes you ain't nearly as funny as you think."

With that, he hung up.

A week later I got a late-night call from him.

"Noon tomorrow, not a minute sooner or later. Park down there on Oglethorpe Street, come through the lot to the back entrance, I'll let you in," Chief Black said. "Try to be inconspicuous, will you?"

"Okay to bring Scotts?"

He hesitated a moment. "Yeah, okay," he said and hung up.

60

WE parked the car on the south end of Oglethorpe Street a few minutes before noon. It was a quiet residential street with small wooden houses set deep on narrow, mostly unkempt lots. There was no one stirring, no one to see us as we walked hastily the four blocks into downtown.

As we neared the courthouse, we heard shouts and taunts coming from above. I looked up and saw the barred windows on the top floor.

"The jail's up there," Scotts said. "On days like today, they open the windows, give the inmates fresh air."

"And a chance to air their grievances."

She rolled her eyes. "Most of them are regulars. They know when to stop or they'll get the windows closed."

"Is that where Lorelei would be?"

"This is the only jail," Scotts said. "It's pretty grungy up there. I can't believe her grandfather's leaving her in that place. Mine did that to me, I'd kill him."

"She's already tried that," I reminded.

We hurried across the lot to the back of the courthouse. There was a ramp that led to a rear metal door. Will Black had said to be there at exactly noon and according to my watch we were on time.

The parking lots on both sides of the courthouse were empty except for Will Black's cop car near the side entrance and a couple of civilian cars in the far corner. It was lunch hour. Will Black apparently saw this as the best chance for us to come and go unseen.

We'd been waiting ten minutes outside the door when we heard a disturbance. At first we thought it was the prisoners above, but a glance up told us the windows had been closed. The noise – rowdy voices – seemed to come and go. They were coming from deep inside the building.

Scotts gave the back door a tug and it opened.

"Did he say wait for him, or were we supposed to go in?" she asked me.

"He said wait until he came to the door."

"He forgot. Let's go, I know where the interview room is."

We stepped in and eased the door closed. The halls were empty. The voices were more distinct, and they weren't having an everyday, genteel Southern jaw. This was a shouting match.

Scotts led us to a wide, windowless corridor with tiled walls and floors. The voices continued to get louder and echo through the hall. There was a sharp crack that sounded like a slap, then a muffled banging noise and a child whimpering.

After the slap, the voice was clear, "Get out of here. You take Robert and leave me alone."

It was a familiar voice: Lorelei Rollings.

Scotts ran toward a door at the end of the corridor and I followed. She pushed the door open and we entered the observation room that looked into the interview room. Will Black was standing in the dark at the two-way mirror, watching intently as Jacob Lacobee and Lorelei glared at one another. They had squared off cheek to cheek as if to fight. The boy stood shivering in one corner, his face pressed to the wall.

Will Black shushed us and waved us over.

"This is getting ugly," he whispered. "Lacobee's slapped her around already. We're not supposed to interfere, but I'm gonna have to stop it if it gets any worse."

Abruptly, Lorelei spun away then jumped right back in Lacobee's face. We all three moved closer to the window.

"He was coming between us, between our family," Lorelei pleaded in a high pitch. "Don't you understand? He was destroying our family!"

Lacobee reached out, took her in his arms and pulled her head to his chest. "You didn't have to do nothing, girl. I coulda took care of him my ownself. He wadn't nothing to worry about, I coulda took care of it," Lacobee said. He stroked her long black hair like a man soothing a raven.

"You listen to me. . . them cops think it was me done it and I ain't letting them think otherwise. You'll be just fine, baby girl."

"I know but. . . but, I didn't do anything," she said in short breaths, sniffling. She clung to him tightly.

The boy, still pressed into the corner, slid down the wall and cowered on the floor, covering his face with his hands.

"Now, now, girl, it's okay," Lacobee said. "We're going to get you home soon. We just gotta get all these lawyer things done, and let that doctor finish seeing to you, then you're coming home."

"That doctor, he's some kind of mental doctor," she said.

"Yeah, he is. But that's okay. He's just looking to see what he can give you to help your nerves, that's all. Just to help your nerves."

"To see if I'm crazy, is what. That's what."

"Just to help your nerves, baby girl. Just to help you nerves." He spoke to her slowly, rhythmically, as he patted her head.

She pulled away from him, her breath short, her eyes flooded with tears. "Where's Robert? Where is he?"

Lacobee looked toward the corner, saw him on the floor and pointed. "Right there. He's right there. He's okay."

She ran over to him, stooped and pulled him up. "Stand up, baby. It's okay. It's okay. Me and Papa were just talkin'. Just talkin' about me coming home so I can take care of you. That's all. It's okay."

She pulled him to her tightly. Lacobee went to them and gently pried the boy away from her. "We're gonna have to go, Lorelei, in just a minute."

"Already? You just got here?"

"No, we been here almost an hour, baby girl."

"Can't you stay longer? I'm so scared."

"Not right now. We gotta go. We gotta hurry and get them papers filed so we can get you out of here." He pointed to a legal document sitting on the table in the center of the room. "Right there. You still have to sign 'em, then we can file 'em."

She stepped over to the table and sat. She stared at the papers with blank eyes. Then she looked up at him.

"Why did you have to kill my Cat?" she said softly.

"I didn't kill Big Cat," he said angrily. "Why did you have to be screwing every thing that lives in Georgia, including practically your own brother? Why that? You want to be asking questions, girl, ask yourself that one."

She jumped up from the table and stepped in his face. "He wasn't my brother! I loved him. I loved my Cat."

"You love every one, girl. From that boy Jimmy Shyne to I don't know who all. That's who prolly killed Cat, that boy Jimmy Shyne."

"No it wasn't. It wasn't him, I know it. It was you! You, you, you!"

Lacobee slapped her with an open palm. "You listen, girl and you listen good. Cat did what he did to protect you. That's what happened. And you better be damn grateful to him for the rest of your life. I talked to him cause we understood each other. I explained to him that as long as he was alive, you were in trouble. Told him he was the one who got you into this mess, now he had to take care of things his ownself."

Lacobee fell silent a moment. He lowered his head and looked off.

"He understood. He was a lot smarter than people took him for."

"You. . .made. . .Cat. . .kill himself? He didn't do anything. He didn't do nothing!"

"No, girl, I didn't *make* him. You, girl, you're the one who brought that on, getting him all involved with you and that Atlanta bunch. You're the one who got Cat killed. You're the one tore the family apart. Bobby Rollings didn't do nothing compared to you. I coulda took care of him my ownself without you interfering."

"I didn't do anything!" She yanked herself away from him and ran to the wall. She buried her face in her hands and sobbed. She was screaming so loud we had to back away from the glass. She banged her fists on the wall and cried out, "Bobby, Bobby, Bobby!"

Lacobee stepped over and pulled the boy to his feet. He took a pen out of his shirt pocket and slammed it on the table.

"There, girl! Now sign them papers on the boy, and you can get outta here and get back to whoring with whoever you damn well please. That's all you want anyway."

She turned to him and screamed, her face a terrifying swirl of fear and anger and hatred.

"I know what those papers are, and you aren't getting him! You aren't getting my son!"

"You're a filthy whore, girl, and I'm giving you what you want, all you want. I'm giving you a way outta here," he sneered at her.

She grabbed the pen on the table and lifted it in the air, wielding it like a knife. The boy turned his face into Lacobee and held onto him in terror.

"You are not taking him! You are not taking him, never!" she cried. "Never! Never!"

She rushed at Lacobee who instinctively pulled the boy up into the protection of his arms. He stumbled back under the weight.

She thrust the pen down, the first strike into her grandfather's arm. Blood spurted out. She cried louder. "You will never have him! Never, never, never!"

She thrust the pen down again, this time hitting the boy in the back. He screamed in pain. She stabbed the boy again. And again. And again. He writhed in screams and blood.

"I will never let you have him!"

Will Black bolted from the observation room.

Lorelei continued to stab at her grandfather and the boy until Will Black burst through the door and body-slammed her across the room into the wall.

Lacobee had fallen to the floor, the boy now limp in his arms.

I looked to Scotts and she was staring at the scene, frozen in disbelief.

"Hey, hey," I said, pulling on her arm. "We need to get help. There has to be someone else in this building. Let's go."

61

Scotts and I spent the rest of the day at the courthouse. They separated us, and both the DA and the Sheriff grilled us then took our formal statements. They spent several hours apparently trying to decide if they would charge us with criminal trespass or some such.

Will Black took the fall, the DA finally told us; he said we were there at his invitation.

Late that evening they released us.

I drove Scotts home. We were both still shaken, not able to find words for a conversation. I offered to walk her to the door, but she said she'd be fine, though she could use a few days off. I agreed that was a good idea for both of us and said I'd call in a few days.

I headed back to Atlanta, assembling on the way the events of the day to report to Mr. Manship. Someone needed to call him and I doubted Will Black would be doing it – he had a lot of explaining to do and could be sitting in a cell right now for all I knew.

I couldn't get the image of the dying kid out of my mind. First Big Cat, now the child. I thought I'd become hardened to death, but I hadn't. Especially not this kind – the kind where you knew the victim. Odd as it sounded, I felt like I'd come to know them both. I knew something about the *other* side of them, the side that was not the *who, what, when, where, and why* of the news story. True, Big Cat had a dark side. And the kid was almost certainly being drawn that way, too. But neither was empty of all humanity, nobody is. Not them, not even Bobby Rollings.

I reached my apartment about midnight and called Mr. Manship's private line. He answered right away, and I told him what had happened.

"The boy is dead?" he asked.

"Died from his wounds on the way to the hospital."

"Jacob Lacobee?"

"In the hospital but stable, we understand."

"Will Black?"

"I don't know, sir. They could be charging him with something. We never talked to him again."

"Lorelei Rollings?"

"They'll have to charge her with murder of some kind. I don't see how they can get around it. Three witnesses – four, if Lacobee survives."

"Call me when you have the full story."

"Yes, sir," I said and hung up.

I fell into bed with a vague sense of dread and not the slightest inclination to sleep. Now it was the image of Lorelei, the madness in her face. And still, even with that, it was the most beautiful face – even to me, one who had watched her murder her own son. The attraction, the magnetism she had – what was that?

What was that?

62

THE next morning I made a spur-of-the-moment decision. I grabbed a taxi over to Manning's Motorcycles and within two hours had settled on a used Triumph – a like-new black Bonneville with only three thousand miles. Hardly broken in.

I rode it home, loaded my saddlebags with camping gear and headed for the Blue Ridge Parkway. I didn't tell anyone where I was going or how long I'd be.

I spent the better part of a week on the bike and in the woods. Humming down the highways and stirring campfires had always soothed my mind in the past. It worked again this time.

I returned home to a phone message from Will Black. He needed me to call him at his house as soon as possible. It sounded urgent, so I did.

He didn't mention the tragedy at the courthouse. He got right to the point: He wanted to know what it was I had to show him. He reminded me that out on the road that day with Mr. Manship, I'd said I had something for him to see.

"Yeah, that's right. But I'm not sure now where it fits—"

"If it was important then, it's important now."

"That's true, Chief, but—"

"No need for that, I'm not Chief. I don't work for the Sheriff's Department."

"Oh, shit."

"It's not a problem. I've got my thirty. I was staying around to run for Sheriff next election. Letting a kid get killed right under my nose ended that idea."

"There *were* circumstances."

He ignored me. "What is it you got?"

"Yeah, okay. It's that graveyard on the plantation, back there where they buried Rollings."

"What about it?"

"Weren't you there for the funeral?"

"Weaver and I went, but we didn't go back to the cemetery. We stayed at the house during the ceremony to keep on eye on things."

"There's a row of unmarked graves back there. Two dozen, maybe more. You'd have seen them."

"So?"

"So, how many missing persons do you have on file at the Sheriff's Office?"

"Not two dozen, if that's what you're suggesting. A few, maybe, in my thirty years."

"What would it take to get those graves dug up? A search warrant, right?"

"A fucking Act of Congress is what. And the old man to die. Neither of which seems likely right now."

"That's what I figured."

"What's this about? There's nothing in that graveyard to tell us who did what to Bobby Rollings."

"No, it's something else."

Will Black fell silent. Either he was waiting for me to say more or he'd lost interest. If he was no longer a cop, I wondered why he'd bothered to call. It wasn't like we had any special connection, though he did seem to have one with Scotts and her family. It occurred to me, though, there were still some gaps in our story, some real ambiguities, and he could help.

"What are you really calling about, Chief?"

"I got a little theory to test. You want to show me those graves or not?" he asked. "This'll be a good time to go while the old man's still in the hospital."

"Yeah, okay. I can show you. There's a back way into the graveyard, a trailhead off FM 71 on the north side. We can meet there and walk in."

"I know where it is. I'll be there at six this evening. And look, son, *do not* bring the girl."

He hung up.

I didn't know what to make of his demand not to bring Scotts – though if he hadn't said anything I probably wouldn't have. But, there it was again. That thing: When people tell you *not* to do something, it stirs the juices of recalcitrance and, worse, spreads the seeds of doubt.

I was at the trailhead at six, as arranged. Will Black pulled up a half-hour later in an old jalopy of a truck. That and his civilian garb threw me for a minute, until he was clear of the truck and his familiar paunch came into full view.

"I'm late," he said as he approached. He rolled the cylinder of the service revolver he'd pulled off the seat of his truck and stuck it in his belt.

"Pest control. You never know," he said with a crooked smile.

We made our way down the trail, back to the cemetery. On the walk in, I told him the origin of the name, DeRussey, and the bit of history Scotts had passed on to me. He said he didn't care.

When we got there, I showed him the trench where Big Cat had been dumping dead hogs and then pointed to the mounds that sat back in the deep shadows of the tree line.

"That's what you think are graves?" he asked.

"That's what they look like."

He circled them a couple of times. He then walked over to the new mound where Big Cat had told the boy his daddy was buried.

"This must be Mr. Rollings."

"Must be," I said.

Will Black spent the next half hour sniffing around the cemetery, moving here and there, poking into the dirt, returning to the unmarked graves a couple of times. He peered down into the trench full of dead hogs.

"Shit, that stinks," he said. "That lime don't quite do the trick."

In time, he drifted back to where I stood.

"So what is it you think we're looking at exactly?" he asked, nodding toward the mounds.

"Manship's brother, Louis. Maybe."

"How's that?"

"You heard what Lacobee said the other day. Louis went missing, over fifty years ago. After accidentally killing the Lacobee boy."

"That's not Mr. Manship's version, as I recall," Will Black said.

"I'm not sure Mr. Manship remembers it right."

I told Will Black what I'd found in the State Archives – the application for a *Declaration of Death* by Louis Manship's own parents.

"Lacobee's version could be closer to the truth," I said.

"Could be, I guess. Things happen to a fifty-year-old memory. Facts have a way of shiftin' around. You'll see soon enough."

"That's what this whole story is about," I said. "At least for Manship. It's about his dead brother."

"Maybe so, maybe not," he said. "Irregardless, what are you intending to do about it?"

"What would you do?"

"Me? I'd do positively nothing," he said. "That's what I'd do. Not a damn thing."

"Leave it alone?"

"I told you what I'd do. I'd leave it lay."

"Yeah, you did say that."

"Sometimes it's don't pay to be right on things the boss is wrong about," he said.

There was a sudden stirring in the underbrush. Will Black looked toward the sound and put his hand on his gun.

"That's wild hogs, Chief. They're all over the place."

"No it ain't," he said. He stepped toward the sound. He stood still for a solid minute then called into the thicket.

"You can come on out of there, Weaver. You been following me a week, now. I know the deal, so let's get this over with."

Will Black stared into the brush, silent.

The brush rustled and Deputy Weaver emerged, in full uniform, his pistol pointed at Will Black.

"What the hell is this?" I said. "What the hell?"

"This is our bad cop," Will Black said. "Right, Weaver?"

"If you say so, Chief," Weaver said.

"I figured you were the one, son."

"Is that so?" Weaver said with a menacing grin. "Never thought you'd be smart enough for that."

"Yeah, but I thought you'd be stupid enough. Man can't hide stupid, no matter how smart he thinks he is."

"Go ahead and drop that old pea-shooter you got on the ground," Weaver said. "Go ahead and do it, now. And you, newspaper man, move on over here next to him."

Weaver held the gun steady on us, not a sign of a wobble in his hand.

"What're you gonna do, shoot us both, throw us in with the dead hogs? That'll be hard to explain. You got a real. . . what do they call it now? A dilemma?" Will Black said.

"I'm not sure what I'm gonna do."

"I tell you, son, that'd be the smart thing to do. Shoot us and dump us."

"Yeah, it would."

"Was she that good, Weaver? Lorelei Rollings? Was she? So damn many of you boys have took the bait, that must be some kind of woman. Is she? Some kinda woman?"

"Yeah, she is. Some kinda woman. Had no idea what I was getting into. Before I knew it, I was in. All in. I wouldn't have done that if I'd known where it was gonna lead. But, hell, here I am now. Here *we* are."

"Yep. Here we are," Will Black said. "I gotta give you credit, though, that was a nice touch – that Easter Sunday business, I mean. Make it look like the old man's crazy hand in it, set him up as the suspect. Threw me off for a while, I can tell you that. Was that your idea or hers?"

"You're kidding, right?"

"Nope."

"Shit, I thought you figured it *all* out," Weaver said.

"Nope. Enlighten me."

"Lorelei. . . well, you don't love her for her mind, you know."

"So I've heard."

"But the fuckin', now that *is* something else."

"Heard that too."

"I wanted it all for myself. Didn't want to share it with Rollings, Cat, Jimmy Shyne or any of the rest."

"So it was all you, Weaver? All you?"

"All me, Chief."

"She thought it was her grandfather," Will Black said.

"Yep."

"He thought it was her."

"I never imagined that working like that, but looks like it did."

"You hired Ardis Cash for the killing, then you set him up. You brought that card into the cabin, stuck it in the purse."

"You're on a roll now, Chief."

"You shot up the motorcycles."

"No, now I had a little help on that. Bad help, it turns out. Dumb fucker couldn't shoot. Didn't quite get the job done."

"Then you killed Big Cat."

"Nope. Now that wasn't me either. I don't know how that happened, but it was a helluva stroke of luck, that's for sure."

"You sayin' that wasn't you?"

"Not me, Chief. Just my good fortune."

"Damn, son. I overestimated you. I was beginning to think you were a genius."

"I'd a made a good cop, Chief. I would have."

"Yeah, you would have. I'm sorry, son."

"A good cop, but not a very good Bad Guy, huh?" Weaver said.

"What the hell, Weaver, what the hell?"

"I don't know, Chief."

"Well, god damn. This breaks my fuckin' heart."

"Mine, too. Mine, too."

"So now what?" Will Black said.

"I don't know. I just don't know."

"Let us help you out, asshole," said Scotts, as she came out of the bushes behind Weaver, cocking her gun at the back of his head. "Drop your gun."

She shouted over her shoulder, "Give me some damn help here, Boyd, will ya for god sake?"

Deputy Boyd O'Con stepped out of the underbrush about twenty feet off to her right, his gun aimed at Weaver as well.

Will Black turned to me, his face twisted in anger.

"What the hell is this? I told you not the bring her. And what's *he* doing here. O'Con, what the hell are *you* doing here?"

"She asked, I came, Chief," O'Con said. "She's my cousin. I had to be sure she was okay, that's all. I had no idea—"

"Well hell no, of course you didn't." Will Black swung his anger back to me. "You didn't trust me? You fuckin' didn't TRUST me?"

"I wasn't sure, goddammit! When you told me not to bring anyone—"

"Jesus H. Christ! It's hard enough living in this world, but when nobody trusts you, it's damn impossible." He took a quick, deep breath then straightened his back. "I'll deal with all three of you later."

"Don't be so damn dramatic, Will Black," Scotts barked at him. "You ain't exactly been Mr. Up-and-Up with us, you know!"

Will Black turned back to Weaver. He had refused to drop his gun, but it was trembling in his hand now. Will Black saw the confusion, the uncertainty in his eyes and heaved a heavy sigh. "God damn, son. Now what? Now we've got a helluva mess. You do, anyhow."

"Yeah, I do. It's a mess," Weaver said, his voice cracking.

"And now it looks like these people with guns gotta decide if they're gonna shoot you or let you turn yourself in. Another goddamn dilemma. I hate those things."

Weaver didn't hesitate. He didn't think about it a moment more. He put his gun to his head. "I'm sorry, Chief. I couldn't resist." He pulled the trigger.

We stood frozen in time, for what seemed forever, but it was just a split second.

"God damn you, Weaver!" Will Black cried out. He leaned over, braced himself on his knees. He took two deep breaths, then pushed himself back upright, turned away from us all and took a few heavy steps away.

"God damn stupid kid," he muttered, then spun and hurried back to the body on the ground.

Boyd O'Con holstered his gun and rushed to the fallen Weaver. He knelt and felt for a pulse.

He gave it a minute then shook his head.

"Nothing, Chief. . .I. . .I. . I think that's it."

"God damn stupid fuckin' kid!" Will Black said and slammed his fist into the fallen Weaver's chest. "Stupid fuckin' kid!"

We all stood in silence a moment. O'Con took a deep breath then said quietly to Will Black, "You know, I'm gonna have to call this in, Chief."

"Course you are, O'Con. Do it," Will Black said, looking up at him solemnly.

O'Con held his gaze. "First, you all need to get out of here. I can explain this. Easy enough. Go on out of here."

"Hell no, O'Con," Will Black said. "We're not gonna do that."

O'Con ignored him. "Weaver called me to meet him here, told me his story, then did this. All nearbouts true. Hell, it *is* true!"

"You can't do that, Boyd," Scotts said.

Will Black shook his head at O'Con. "No, son, you can't do that."

"Yes I can, Chief." He looked again at Will Black.

Will Black looked off.

"I damn sure can, Chief! Now go on. Get the hell out of here, all of you. It's gonna come out the same way whether you're here or not. So, go on, get out of here. I got this."

We hesitated.

"I'm serious. Get the hell out of here," O'Con said.

Will Black looked at Weaver a moment and shook his head. Then he turned to us. "Let him handle it. C'mon."

We hurried the mile back to the road in silence, listening to Boyd O'Con talk to the dispatcher, his voice growing more faint with each step we took.

63

DEPUTY O'Con had little trouble convincing the DA that Weaver's death was a suicide. The forensics confirmed it, and the evidence of the connection between Weaver and Lorelei – which Will Black had been collecting and had left on file – was considerable. It supported Boyd O'Con's version of events and the confession he claimed Weaver had made.

Will Black had suspected Weaver from the outset. His actions at the Rollings murder scene had been uncharacteristically anxious and careless for what Black considered his best cop. Soon after, Weaver had inserted himself onto the crew assigned to keep an eye on Scotts and I – a job Will Black had specifically given the part-timers to handle. When I told Will Black I'd seen Weaver watching my apartment in Atlanta, he suspected then that Weaver was running astray.

He had Weaver tailed by an ex-deputy. He'd been observed at Jimmy Shyne's club, at Lorelei's house, and in two meetings with Ardis Cash. Black then had Weaver's bank records pulled and found several thousand-dollar cash withdrawals in the months prior to the Rollings murder.

And when Scotts and I were ambushed and Weaver was conveniently nearby, Black knew that he had no business being out that way that night. No police business, anyway.

Despite all that, Will Black hadn't wanted to believe Weaver was part of the Rollings killing, only that he'd been snared in Lorelei's web. That's why he had taken Lorelei's purse into Big Cat's cabin and left it for Weaver to find – the purse he'd already examined and knew the contents of. The purse that *did not* contain Jimmy Shyne's business card with Ardis Cash's name on back.

After Lorelei killed her son and Will Black was fired, Weaver began to unravel. He had begun following Will Black almost everywhere. Carelessly. Openly.

Will Black figured it was only a matter of time before he came unhinged. Which, in fact, he did. In DeRussey.

64

WILL Black never faced any charges in connection with the death of the child. As he put it, "I know too much about too many for anyone to get self-righteous. A clean slate was part of my retirement package."

And in the weeks that followed, he was more than helpful to us in filling in the holes in the Bobby Rollings story. We met several times at Drigger's Bar and he provided not only updates on the case – inside info he was still able to get from O'Con – but facts and insights in the investigation that only he, as lead investigator, had had.

In our last meeting, he told us he had a job interview in the private sector that looked promising. We wished him well and meant it.

Scotts and I spent several more weeks cobbling together the full story for Mr. Manship. We prepared a newspaper version in the event he wanted to publish it. We were not able to present it to him immediately, though. He had been pulled away by the demands of several new media acquisitions on the west coast.

Before leaving town, though, he had put Scotts on the *Democrat* staff full time and sent both of us to the newspaper's Special Assignments unit known as *The Enterprise Team*. He assured us it was a temporary assignment, that he would have another inquiry for us soon.

The Enterprise Team we joined, interestingly, was investigating the rampage of apparent arson-for-profit fires in the Fourth Ward. We were able to contribute significantly right away.

65

In late August I finally received a call from Mrs. Christian setting up a meeting with Mr. Manship. She said he had asked that I bring Mrs. Scott. He had instructed her to say that he was ready for the full story. The meeting would be at his residence at 9:30 p.m. Sunday. She asked if she should have any special beverage on hand for Mrs. Scott, and I told her ginger ale was her beverage of choice.

We were there promptly at nine p.m. and were invited to wait in a small sitting area until 9:30, because, it seems, I had misunderstood her clear instructions to be there at 9:30, not nine.

"I'm certain I misunderstood, Mrs. Christian," I said. "My apologies."

Scotts and I both took a seat and cooled our heels.

At exactly 9:30 she took us back to Mr. Manship's study. He was seated in his usual spot. Across from him was a familiar face: Will Black.

Both men stood and welcomed us. Then we all sat.

"I wanted you to meet the new Head of Security for Manship Media," Mr. Manship said to us. He gestured toward Will Black. "I think you all know each other."

"Yes, sir, we do."

Will Black looked like a new man. He was almost spiffy. His graying hair was neatly trimmed, his face clean-shaven, and he'd dropped enough weight to fit comfortably into a nice blue-and-white seersucker suit. I wouldn't call him corporate yet, but he was getting close.

Scotts beamed at the news. She had always liked Will Black, had never once doubted him or his commitment to his job. I had been a late convert but had come to see that not only did his bumpkin mannerisms conceal a brilliant intelligence, there was also a streak of decency running through him a mile wide.

"I wanted you to be the first to know," Mr. Manship said to Scotts and I. "Because you will all be working closely together on our next inquiry. And it's an interesting one. I believe you'll find it so. But first, anything to drink?"

Mrs. Christian served us and we settled in to tell him the story.

"Before you start, do you mind if Mr. Black stays?" Mr. Manship asked. "He has something to tell us when you're finished."

We said of course he should stay, it was his story, too.

"Good. Tell us, then," he said. He sat back in his chair, relaxed his shoulders and reached for his cigar.

We told him the entire story – the one you have just read, with only minor omissions – from beginning to end. He listened carefully to every detail, studied every nuance of word or phrase we used. Will Black sat stoic, listening and quietly nodding agreement from time to time.

As we drew to the end of the story, we summarized the current status:

Lorelei Rollings was still in the hospital – a long-term psychiatric care unit in Atlanta. When released – which was not likely to be anytime soon – she would face charges of first-degree manslaughter in the death of her son. She was, according to staff on the unit, virtually catatonic. Her few attempts to communicate were incomprehensible – "salad talk" they called it.

Her son, Robert Rollings, III, was buried in DeRussey, the family cemetery on Montrose Plantation. His grave was next to where his great-grandfather would one day be buried.

Leon "Big Cat" Metoyer's death had been ruled a suicide by the Latham County Coroner. He, too, was buried in DeRussey, very close to where Lacobee would lay.

We were all confident – Will Black included – that Lacobee's admission to Lorelei that he had lead Big Cat to kill himself was truthful. We believed Big Cat's ultimate loyalty was to Lorelei, that he had loved her like nothing else in the world, and that it would not have taken much for Lacobee to convince him to die to save her.

"That was the tragedy in all this, sir," Scotts added. "Cat loved Lorelei like none of the rest did; and if she could love anyone, it was him."

Will Black nodded solemn agreement.

I went on: A small-time hood from the Fourth Ward by the name of Ronnie Lee Brown had been arrested for pulling the trigger in the Bobby Rollings murder.

His name had been found among Deputy John Weaver's effects.

Under questioning, Brown broke and confessed that Ardis Cash had been the man who hired him to kill Bobby Rollings. Cash had given him the shotgun, the shells and a yellow Cadillac to use. Ardis Cash had assured him there was no chance he'd get caught because the job was for a cop. Cash had given him specific instructions on exactly how and when to kill Bobby Rollings. He described the morning of the killing in detail.

Ronnie Lee Brown had been paid one thousand dollars for the job.

Brown also confessed to ambushing us. That had been arranged personally by Deputy John Weaver. Ardis Cash had put Brown and Weaver in direct contact after the killing and told them he was no longer their middle man, he was getting out of town.

Brown was supposed to have killed Scotts and I and left us on the road. Weaver was going to find the bodies and clean up any evidence left behind. But, Brown added, he had never been a very good shot, so he missed the riders, killed the motorcycles.

Jimmy Shyne, as far as the cops could find, was never anything more than one of Lorelei's paramours. His name was barely noted in any police report and had not been mentioned in any news reporting of the case.

Jacob Lacobee had been hospitalized almost two weeks for the half-dozen stab wounds Lorelei had inflicted. There had been some infections but none had seriously threatened him. When he was released from the hospital, he was charged with obstruction. It was a flimsy charge that few thought had any chance of sticking – nor had been intended to stick.

Lacobee was free on his own recognizance and back at his plantation. There were rumors that the plantation was going to seed and that the old man had lost interest, that he was downcast and despondent. It was a fact that he had not been seen at the First Baptist Church since his great-grandson's funeral. And it was a fact that he had let many of his plantation hands go. What got done around there now, it appeared, he was doing mostly himself.

We concluded with that.

We told Mr. Manship that was all we had, that was the story as it stood right now.

He looked at Scotts a moment, smiled and nodded his appreciation. He did the same to me.

"You say you have a written version? A story for the paper?"

"Yes sir. It would need a good edit. Maybe an update, depending on when it runs," I said, and added quickly, "*If* it runs."

"Leave it for me, I want to read it."

Scotts handed him the story, all two hundred pages of it. He held it in his hand and considered its heft. Then he leafed through it for a moment or two.

"Are there any more copies of this?" he asked.

"Yes, sir," I said.

"There shouldn't be. See to that, if you would."

"Yes, sir, I will."

He placed the story on his side table and turned to Will Black. "You said you had something?"

"Yes, sir, I do."

"Okay." He gestured for Will Black to proceed.

Will Black nodded and addressed Mr. Manship directly.

"Jacob Lacobee was found dead today, a little after noon. He was found laying in the middle of his cotton field. His tractor was there, still running, right beside him. It appears he fell off, hit his head on the trailing implement, and died on the spot. No one was around. He was out plowing his field himself."

He gave us a look of irony, opened his palms. "That's what they found, two of the field hands he still had working for him."

Mr. Manship raised his eyes and stared at Will Black. He was startled by the news. He had clearly not seen it coming. Will Black must have told him earlier only that he had something to report, not what it was.

Scotts had gasped softly, put one hand to her mouth and cut her eyes to me. I returned her look and said nothing.

We sat silent for several minutes, rolling the news over in our minds. "No foul play, then?" Mr. Manship asked at last.

Will Black's face was impassive. He sat stony as a statue, without a hint of emotion. If he was intending to guard some secret, he was doing it well.

"No, sir. No foul play," Will Black said.

"You're sure about that?"

"My friends in the department assure me that's the case, yes, sir. No foul play. Accidental death."

"I see," Mr. Manship said. He turned his gaze to the wide window overlooking Atlanta and stared out into the twinkling skyline. After a moment, a crease of a smile crept across his face. He glanced at his watch then rose. He walked to his desk. He sat down, breathed a slow, heavy sigh and looked over at the three of us.

His eyes seemed to be saying that he had lost something – that thing he had despised most and hated for so long and yet needed with equal fervor. It was the story he had not been ready to end and yet now would have to.

"We'll have to discuss our next inquiry tomorrow, if you don't mind," he said. "Will you have Mrs. Christian show you out?" He reached across the desk for his pen.

"I want to write Jacob Lacobee's obituary myself."

Moments later, the three of us – Will Black, Scotts and I – stood in the hallway outside Mr. Manship's door to say our goodnights.

"I see you decided to leave those DeRussey graves undisturbed," Will Black said.

"For the time being," I said.

"With Lacobee gone, they may be able to dig, you know," he said.

"Maybe so. We're not dropping this."

"No, we're not," he said.

Scotts told Will Black how happy we were to be working with him again. She gave him a huge hug and thanked him once more for all his help. She was a little gushy for my taste – and Will Black's too, from the look on his face – but she was sincere, she had a big heart. Probably even bigger than Will Black's, though neither of them would want word on the size of their hearts to get out.

"What's in those graves you think?" Scotts asked Will Black.

"Same thing that's in any grave: Reality catching up."

He said goodbye and headed for the elevator.

Scotts told him we were taking the stairs down. We turned and walked to the other end of the hall. As we approached the stairwell, she stopped. She had that odd head tilt, that completely puzzled look she had so perfected.

"I have to ask. . . what happened to Lacobee? What was Will Black saying in there? Did somebody kill him or what?"

I looked into those incurably curious eyes of hers.

"Anything possible to be imagined is an image of the truth," I said.

"What? What the hell? Is that supposed to answer my question?"

"That's what Mr. Manship says. I can't do better."

I pushed open the door to the stairwell and started down the stairs ahead of her. In two seconds she had caught up.

"Hey, wait up, Coates. You want to run to Drigger's or something? To celebrate?"

"Not tonight. I have somewhere I need to be."

"Whoa! So you and the DA lady? On again?"

"Maybe."

"Good. Maybe now you won't be so bitchy. But, look, I know you don't like to hug or anything. . . but, don't you think? This time? This once?"

I stopped on the landing. "You know, you're right. And, what do you mean? I like to hug as much as anybody."

We embraced. There was a physical warmth about her. It went with her personal warmth. Mr. Manship knew it almost the instant he met her. She was one of those who, as he said, "got it." Not only did she get it, she had it: A bigness of heart that reached out, reached for your own heart and invited it in.

"Damn good work, partner. Damn good," I said.

She pulled her head back, looked and smiled. "Yeah, you too, partner. Damn good."

We broke the hug and continued down the stairs.

On the very next flight, she said, "You know, there was one other thing I was wondering about—"

"Not now, not now, will you? Enough for one night."

"Yeah, okay, okay. Jeeez, I was just going to ask about our next assignment. But, never mind," she said.

We continued down the remaining flights, in step stride for stride.

Epilogue

Influential Cotton Farmer
Dies in Plantation Accident

Page Three: *The Atlanta Democrat, August 19, 1988*

NEW BETHANY, Ga. – Lifelong cotton farmer and influential voice for agriculture, Jacob Lacobee, died yesterday in an accident on his plantation just outside of New Bethany, Georgia. He was 71 years old.

Lacobee was found dead mid-afternoon after he apparently fell from his tractor and struck his head, according to authorities. He had been clearing a cotton field.

Lacobee was the owner and operator of the state's largest independent cotton farm, known as Montrose Plantation – a 17,000-acre spread that has consistently been named one of the most successful in the country.

He is survived by his wife of fifty-one years, Eva Talley Lacobee, and one granddaughter Lorelei Lacobee Rollings. He is preceded in death by both his parents, one son and one great-grandson.

Lacobee was longtime chairman of the Georgia Independent Growers Association and served on the Board of Directors of two banks, the Georgia Commerce Bank and the Peoples Bank & Trust of New Bethany. He also served on the Republican National Committee, representing Georgia, and had been a longtime and influential member of the Georgia State Republican Committee.

While lauded as one of state's top producers and twice awarded the National Cotton Council Distinguished Farm Award, Lacobee had his share of legal difficulties over the years.

The Georgia Agricultural Oversight Board had repeatedly cited the farm's reluctance to adopt modern planting, disease control and safety measures as dangerous to workers and to crops. The Board twice levied heavy fines for negligent practices.

Lacobee refused to pay both times and legal challenges to the fines were still underway. There are also four current legal challenges to Lacobee's claim to ownership of sizable tracts of land currently in production on Montrose Plantation. Those challenges have been working through the courts for almost three years.

Lacobee had gained the reputation among his harshest critics as a cruel overlord, running his farm and two cotton ginning mills with an iron hand, never reluctant to use intimidation tactics.

Earlier this year, he was implicated in the murder of his grandson-in-law, Robert Rollings, Jr. Though he was not charged with the murder, he still faced charges of obstruction of justice in connection with the case. Lacobee was also questioned in the death over fifty years ago of Louis Henry Manship, though no charges were ever filed.

Funeral services for Lacobee have not been set but are expected to be held this weekend. Influential members of the agricultural and business communities from across the state, along with members of both state and national political establishments, are expected to be in attendance.

With Gratitude

This book would be incomplete without words of thanks to those who have helped bring it together.

I start with my wife, Mar'Sue, who has endured sweetly all the ups and downs of the process.

I'm likewise grateful to Judy Christie and husband Paul, Michael Henry, Roger Lebrescu and George Sewell for their encouragement and words of writerly advice.

Thanks, too, to Richard Wadsack for permission to borrow a few lines from his personal letters. And a tip of the hat to designers Jim Huckabay and Kevin Martin for cover art, as well as to Steve Passiouras at Bookow for typesetting.

As important as anything to a story is its reader's response, and for their comments on this one, I am indebted to: Michael Henry, George Sewell, John Haigler, Roger Lebrescu, Lisa Welby, Nina Hustus, Amy McDonald, Jim Huckabay, Judith Wilson and Judy Christie.

Finally, a word of thanks to the people of this story. We all understand, of course, that this book is fiction and that its people are fictitious characters. Invariably, though, these fictions come alive to the author (and hopefully to the reader) and this cast has performed well, has been especially lively. So, to Mr. Manship, Gil Coates, Emily Scott, Will Black, Calvin Daniels, Jimmy Shyne, Lacey Moore, Jacob Lacobee, Big Cat, and Lorelei Rollings, thank you. And encore! We'll have to have you back for more. Well, some of you.

–Jim Wilson

Contact

The author appreciates hearing from readers.

Please contact him via email at:

JamesLWilsonAuthor@gmail.com

www.ingramcontent.com/pod-product-compliance
Lightning Source LLC
Chambersburg PA
CBHW030004290326
41934CB00005B/214